D0794161

About Island Press

Since 1984, the nonprofit Island Press has been stimulating, shaping, and communicating the ideas that are essential for solving environmental problems worldwide. With more than 800 titles in print and some 40 new releases each year, we are the nation's leading publisher on environmental issues. We identify innovative thinkers and emerging trends in the environmental field. We work with world-renowned experts and authors to develop cross-disciplinary solutions to environmental challenges.

Island Press designs and implements coordinated book publication campaigns in order to communicate our critical messages in print, in person, and online using the latest technologies, programs, and the media. Our goal: to reach targeted audiences—scientists, policymakers, environmental advocates, the media, and concerned citizens—who can and will take action to protect the plants and animals that enrich our world, the ecosystems we need to survive, the water we drink, and the air we breathe.

Island Press gratefully acknowledges the support of its work by the Agua Fund, Inc., Annenberg Foundation, The Christensen Fund, The Nathan Cummings Foundation, The Geraldine R. Dodge Foundation, Doris Duke Charitable Foundation, The Educational Foundation of America, Betsy and Jesse Fink Foundation, The William and Flora Hewlett Foundation, The Kendeda Fund, The Andrew W. Mellon Foundation, The Curtis and Edith Munson Foundation, Oak Foundation, The Overbrook Foundation, the David and Lucile Packard Foundation, The Summit Fund of Washington, Trust for Architectural Easements, Wallace Global Fund, The Winslow Foundation, and other generous donors.

The opinions expressed in this book are those of the author(s) and do not necessarily reflect the views of our donors.

THE NATURE OF A HOUSE

GEORGE M. WOODWELL

THE NATURE OF A HOUSE

Building a World that Works

ISLANDPRESS

Washington | Covelo | London

Library of Congress Cataloging-in-Publication Data

Woodwell, G. M.
   The nature of a house : building a world that works / George M. Woodwell.
      p.   cm.
   Includes bibliographical references and index.
   ISBN-13: 978-1-59726-558-4 (cloth : alk. paper)
   ISBN-10: 1-59726-558-6 (cloth : alk. paper)   1. Ecological houses.   2. Dwellings—Remodeling.   3. Sustainable living.   I. Title.
   TH880.W663   2009
   720'.47—dc22
                                   2009021549

Printed on recycled, acid-free paper

Manufactured in the United States of America
10 9 8 7 6 5 4 3 2 1

KEYWORDS: Green building; green office space; green renovation; energy conservation; climate change; Woods Hole, Massachusetts; The Woods Hole Research Center; William McDonough; Hilltop House; wind energy; solar energy; natural sewage treatment

CONTENTS

FOREWORD

As an architect, I think about design as the first signal of human intention. If this is true in any way, then George Woodwell is a consummate designer. George sees, gimlet-eyed, into the science of the effects that humans have on nature. He sees the science in the broadest sense and then moves to render visible the change he wishes to see in the world. One delightful manifestation of George's vision, perspicacity, and design is the Ordway Campus of the Woods Hole Research Center, a small complex of buildings and landscapes where researchers discover not only what is wrong is about humans in the world but also what behaviors might set things right. This is a place of wonder and healing for an increasingly distressed planet.

Just what makes the Ordway Campus such a special place? Imagine a place that generates more energy than it needs to operate, where every drop of water has been considered for the productive health it brings to the ecosystem. Imagine buildings like trees—they capture photosynthetic energy, as well as energy from the wind and the earth. Imagine buildings made of silica, carbohydrates, and metals, designed for a long useful life followed by their safe return to biological or technical nutrient flows. Such buildings show how we can conduct a creative and principled dialogue with Earth that generates a living architecture for our time—a technologically sophisticated, aesthetically rich language that celebrates people and place, community and creativity, sunlight and landscape. Imagine these goals for a project—lofty indeed, but achievable in the lifetime of a visionary like George Woodwell.

We work with many good people who are trying to make their organizations and places more efficient and less bad. They are working toward a "zero goals." They are willing to stop there. But being "as efficient as possible" was never the goal of the Woods Hole Research Center at Ordway Campus. George, like us, was relentlessly seeking a higher purpose by design. He was seeking a world where we are are effective, not just efficient—one where we celebrate the positive effects of renewable energies.

We at William McDonough + Partners see this as the act of a true leader. As the late business genius Peter Drucker said, being efficient—doing things right—is the critical role of the manager. But it is the leader's job to be effective—to see that the "right things get done." We realize that efficiently managing a toxic system could never be the right thing. But effective innovations within a life-affirming design protocol suggest a dynamic path to a cradle to cradle world. In this context, George Woodwell is clearly a world leader.

So read this book, wonder at the story of this marvelous journey, and recognize the healing act that it represents—a celebration of human creativity and the abundance of a planet fused with the goodwill of its people.

—*William A. McDonough, FAIA, Int. FRIBA*

ACKNOWLEDGMENTS

Many friends and professional colleagues have contributed infinite details over the years to the story of the Woods Hole Research Center and its new campus, recounted in outline here. The book, however, was my own initiative that originated in a desire to capture for local interest details of the development of the idea, the roles of the people, and the ultimate construction and occupation of the new campus. There were many conversations and key decisions, meetings and missteps over years before we settled finally on the place and the course we would follow. Trustees were key, all under the leadership of Lawrence Huntington, who made his extraordinary talents universally available over a decade that spanned the September 11th tragedy, which was closer to him than most know, and the period of soaring real estate prices that drove us out of Woods Hole to Quissett and a grand new campus there. The initial plan expanded from a booklet of local interest to a larger work of more general interest under the influence of trustees, including especially long-term friend, Merloyd Lawrence, and editors at Island Press. There Heather Boyer took a heavy hand and tried hard to refocus a meandering style into a straightforward and logical book about a building as I fought to diverge into an elaboration of an ecologist's worldview and how to make the world work as a small and threatened biophysical system on the verge of irreversible decay. I owe her a big debt of gratitude for her patience and persistence and logic and for her experience in what works in publishing and what does not. The failures in logic and diversions into lectures on ecology, where they are repetitive and disruptive, are all mine, products of bone-headed persistence against experienced advice.

Katharine Woodwell, who has made my life easy and thoroughly enjoyable over more than fifty years, and who had a powerful administrative role in building the Woods Hole Research Center and the design and construction and occupancy of the building, has also had more to do with clarity and precision in thought and deed of all the participants than she knows. Spare of words, quick of humor, unflappable, she had us all dancing regularly to a delightfully constructive tune.

I have consulted many over the years in which we have conducted this experiment. Dennis Dinan joined our staff from Avon Old Farms School and from many years at Dartmouth and brought a relentlessly systematic and imaginative approach to fund-raising and his own personal brilliance to writing and editing. Gilman Ordway and Gordon Russell, both trustees, displayed early confidence in the plans and programs of the Center and offered major intellectual and financial support. And I was fortunate in being able to call on longtime friends from science and conservation to serve on our board: John Adams, Steve Curwood, Thomas Lovejoy, Victoria Lowell, Mary Lou Montgomery, Lily Rice Hsia, Wilhelm Merck, Amy Regan, Joseph Robinson, Tedd Saunders, Helen Spaulding, Ola Ullsten, Sarah Brown, Jim MacNeill, Ross Sandler, and Gus Speth, as well as John Holdren, who ultimately brought his vigor and extraordinary competence to the directorate as I moved on to emeritus status.

Michael Ernst, Joe Hackler, Tom Stone, Greg Fiske, and Allison White all helped with various aspects of the details of this book. And I have talked with and leaned on the experience of many others, including Fred Palmer, Judy Fenwick, Kilaparti Ramakrishna, Jennifer Gaines, and the Woods Hole Historical Society as well as the Woods Hole Library.

It was a special pleasure to work with Bill McDonough and his architectural colleagues, especially Mark Rylander, who was our principal architect, and their consultant and our friend, energy expert Marc Rosenbaum of Energysmiths.

All have been most generous, including a series of readers who have offered a range of valuable comments and recommendations. Omissions and failures are not their's but mine alone.

PREFACE

A Small Matter of Habitat and Housing

Cassandra sits in high places today.
— John Sloan Dickey, President of Dartmouth College,
addressing the Great Issues course in 1950

I undertake this writing more than fifty-five years after hearing John Sloan Dickey discuss with graduates of Dartmouth College the hazards of life in the new political context of a nuclear-armed world, then only five years old. We have not outlived the nuclear threat, but we have survived it. We have survived to encounter an additional set of biophysical environmental challenges that are in fact far worse than threats. They are transitions in the earth's systems that systematically undermine the human habitat even as human numbers and needs for resources soar. The threat of a nuclear Armageddon continues, worse in many ways for the spread of weapons into the hands of rogue states, combined with the emergence of new rogues from once responsible states. But, so far, it remains a threat, not a reality, despite the periodic eruption of irresponsibility among the nuclear-armed nations. In contrast, the erosion of the global human habitat has become reality and scientists now recognize that, unless we can make drastic changes immediately in this fossil fuel–powered civilization, we shall find ourselves quickly, year-by-year, on a new, increasingly unstable and hostile planet, a disaster no less final than the nuclear Armageddon we have feared for so long.

Even that thought, simple as it seems, has had a long gestation and will be developed further as experience accumulates from experiments such as the one described here as the Woods Hole Research Center explored how well it could do during the very first years of the new millennium in constructing its new campus within the famous scientific community of Woods Hole. It is not adaptation to an irreversibly eroding environment. It is a cure, boiling up from the bottom with all the optimism and vigor of science. Not muddling through, but actively reaching for a big step into the new world we have to envision and build. We are not alone in envisioning a major transition in human affairs, but our emphasis, in contrast to the social and political stirring that Hawken has defined so eloquently,[1] is on the biophysical core and keeping it functional.

I

BUILDING A WORLD THAT WORKS

She had a giant puffball, a fungus from the woods, fully ten inches in diameter, white with traces of brown, on a platter. She had opened the door of Hilltop House to our knock. It was midmorning, but she was in her nightgown, absorbed in admiration for her find, which she announced was on its way to The Café Budapest, her Boston restaurant. There was no question. Livia Hedda Rev-Kury had one of the world's wonders on a platter, a product of the forested eight-acre tract we had just arranged to buy as the new campus of the Woods Hole Research Center. I could not but admire her knowledge that there are no poisonous puffballs and her confidence that this monster was at that early, meaty, edible stage, well before the spores that are the puffball's real business had started to form. Spores make poor eating but a wonderful display as they emerge in an explosive cloud for a reproductive celebration that justifies the puffball name and spreads the fungus around the world. We admired the puffball, a saprophyte, slow growing, expanding toward the moment that is difficult to ignore when its millions of spores flood the world. It was an apt analogy as we set out in 1998 on a new phase in our mission of seeding the world with the new insights into the science of ecology and the political support for the massive transition from a fossil-fueled and failing world to a solar-powered and infinitely renewable world that can serve indefinitely as a human habitat.

The puffball had appeared at the right moment to add to the excitement surrounding our central purpose and the opportunity we saw in testing our own principles through the transformation of Hilltop House into a model for the new world. No matter how much we dream or wish it otherwise, we have but one habitat, and it is now eroding under the ever larger demands of an expanding human presence. Where are we headed in this complex but finite world? Is there but one direction, the continued erosion of the human future?

It need not be so. Does not an environment that is fully supportive of the public interest lie at the core purpose of both science and government? That was our vision, polished over years as we built research programs in ecology in the Woods Hole Research Center and before. Our vision took on new vigor as we contemplated reunification on a single campus. Here we might build anew using the principles of ecology that we develop and honor and set as an example for a world under siege from cumulative local failures. Changing the global course requires both top-down and bottom-up leadership, local revolutions, cumulative, contagious, local successes that silently enter the public realm and erupt into a new world.

The complexity of the global crises of environment is real enough, but the problems are far from impossible. Central among them is growth. Growth in human numbers, growth in demands on all resources—water, air, space, forests, food, shelter, and energy; growth, fed by an insatiable demand for more in every aspect of the human economy. The growth has been enabled by explosive industrial development built on cheap and abundant fossil fuel energy—coal, oil, and, most recently, gas. The combination of cheap energy and industrial genius has seemed capable of solving all problems and of allowing boundless expansion of the human undertaking. Growth has become the touchstone of success in business and in government throughout the capitalist, greed-driven, western world. As we have continued to honor growth in the present context, we have in effect denied the limits of the earth and set a course that changes the earth out from under this civilization. The future promises a progressively dysfunctional and impoverished world.[1] That is the urgent message of the moment brought home by the details of the climatic disruption as they emerge as the final limit to the fossil fuel age from beneath the fraying canopy of industrial expansion and apparent successes. Suddenly, the world is again small and fragile and seriously threatened as biophysical limits—always real, but long ignored—become conspicuous.

Scientists and others have a big job now in leading this transition. We, the staff and trustees of the Woods Hole Research Center, found ourselves in a position to rebuild a small part of the world in a new context consistent with our own dreams of reality for the next century. Our experience was limited, of course. It always is in such ventures. But we were acutely aware of earlier fumbles, the speed of the erosion of the human circumstance, and the magnitude and importance of the challenge. Energy lay at the core, but we were trapped as a part of the fossil-fueled world at the moment. We could aspire to change, but could not march abruptly out of this world into another.

Most important is the realization that the world is the sum of its parts and a world in trouble is in trouble because its parts are not working properly. Correction begins with the parts, each of which must be rebuilt into working order. Our campus is but one of those parts. It must be a model, a contagious inspiration, a giant step in the direction of Ian McHarg's exhortation: *design with nature.*[2]

This book chronicles, through my own eyes and experience, what we saw and learned in the reconstruction and expansion of Hilltop House (figure 1.1) and its eight-acre campus (soon expanded to nine acres by a gift) as an example of the world we need to produce over the next decades.

The immediate objective of course was the consolidation of the activities of staff then scattered among five different sites in Woods Hole into one place that offered not only propinquity and efficiency but also joy and convenience and even beauty and pride of place and purpose. The joy and convenience and beauty and pride and purpose were major issues, for our business is global biophysics—defining and challenging, if possible, the environmental problems of an eroding global environment. And we are closely bound, individually and institutionally, to the industrial society that

Figure 1.1   Hilltop House at the time of purchase by the Woods Hole Research Center in 1998.

is the cause of the erosion. Although there are many causes of the environmental decline, the overwhelmingly important issue is the climatic disruption, a direct product of reliance on fossil fuels. Is it possible for the institution to have a campus that moves into the next age, the postcarbon world, and survives? We thought so, but could we afford it? How far could we go? How would we determine whether to raze and rebuild or to remodel the existing structure? Would there be interest from supporters, architects, builders, and donors? And would we be able to live with the outcome? The need we saw was for an example for the world.

Hilltop House, attractive as it was as a spacious home, presented an immediate dilemma. It was an 1877 relic of an earlier era, the wood-fired, locally self-sufficient era, with a fireplace in every room and a large wood-range in the kitchen. The central oil-fired steam heating system was an afterthought with a boiler built into a pit dug into the basement floor. It was a wooden building, neglected, somewhat shabby. There was a serious question as to whether the original Victorian summer mansion of 1877 vintage should be razed or might easily be modified and expanded to accommodate the new purposes and the innovations in construction and architecture that we saw as part of the transformation. There were several issues, including the question of structural integrity, our own fundamentally conservative interests in reusing an existing structure, and the local political interest in preserving a spectacular and widely known mansion with an interesting history. The building was not, however, an architectural gem. It was not especially well built, contained no special woodwork worthy of note or preservation. Although it was not in the designated historic district of Woods Hole, local interest in preserving ancient buildings favored preserving this conspicuous part of a trio of mansions on Quissett Ridge, two miles north of the village of Woods Hole. Our own New England roots also favored preservation and reuse over demolition, and several surveys of the structure were carried out to determine whether it was sufficiently sound to be preserved and modified for the needs of the Center.

The conclusion of experts was that the building was sound enough to be preserved, which was the more desirable choice from an environmental standpoint, and that it would establish the place and form and style of the segment of the new building that was visible from the road. The decision brought relief in many quarters and general approbation from friends and donors locally.

Excited at the prospect of turning our scientific principles into a practical demonstration appropriate to our history in science, our current work, and our dreams, we marched on with confidence that we could restore the building without great difficulty. If we did our work properly, lived up to our chance, we could use our building not only to explore the frontiers of architecture but also to define what is possible now in turning principles of ecology, and dreams of the essential transitions that the world must make, into reality.

A short time after the purchase in October 1998 I sat with our staff in second- (or fourth-) hand folding chairs in the large front room of Hilltop

House and heard the distinguished architect Bill McDonough expound on how he would help us build "with silica and cellulose" a beautifully comfortable institutional Center that, when it decayed finally after a century or two, would leave no noxious residue at all. The new building would be as a "leaf, reaching out into the forest nearby." Not at all taken in by this hyperbole we could not be anything but impressed with the imagination and flair of Bill McDonough. We talked with other excellent architects, but none had carried the environmental challenges as far, reflected our needs in science as faithfully, or captured us with imaginative pictures and figures of speech and phrases as Bill. And he was well known, brilliantly articulate, and could help us with the fund-raising, which would be critical as the cost of the building rose with every new principle and each new idea.

Despite the excitement of setting forth to design a new headquarters, we could not set aside our core business of research and analysis of the global environment as we sorted through our potential for bringing what we think we know about the world to bear on this new building that we shall live with for the next decades. We were acutely aware that we lived, then and now, in a world that is not working properly as a result of the cumulative effects of earlier failures in design and is in fact in crisis as it becomes less stable daily. The obvious, immediate, acute global failure is the climatic disruption, the quite predictable, and predicted, product of changes in the atmosphere from the massive ongoing combustion of fossil fuels and from reductions in the area of forests globally. The climatic change is already disruptive of civilization through destabilization of agriculture and water supplies, through a rising sea level, intensified storms, and other inconveniences. But the most serious disruption is indirect through a major contribution to the biotic impoverishment of the earth and the normal functions of the environment.[3] That issue is complicated and confounded with other causes of impoverishment, including the toxification of air, water, and land with industrial and other noxious substances, some of which are distributed deliberately, such as poisons to control pests. These are Great Issues and we were privileged to work on them, first in their definition, then in their resolution. Our objective in science and our institutional purpose is to keep the living world safe from further environmental impoverishment. Do we have any potential at all for dealing with this heavy burden in this new project? We do, of course, for our segment is a part of the global sum. And our interest is in the full range of cause and effect and cure.

The core of the public purpose must lie, at least as we saw the world, in preservation of the integrity of function of the biosphere, including the whole of the human environment. That objective requires preserving the physical and chemical, and therefore the biological, integrity of the earth, locally and globally. It is a demanding objective at this stage in civilization, for it requires restoration as opposed to mere restraint. How are we to build within new limits that proscribe the use of fossil fuels and demand materials that do not further poison the earth in either their use or their ultimate decay? The era of explosive "growth" was clearly over, at least as we saw the world, although politicians and economists did not then, and do not now, share the perspective. The cost of that persistence promises to be very great.

The wages of "growth" as pursued in the contemporary context are with us now as the human population, which has doubled in the last forty years and quadrupled in the lifetimes of many now living, continues to expand.[4] The world is afflicted with an accelerating global climatic disruption, rampant biotic impoverishment to the point where fisheries have disappeared and virtually all are threatened, forests over vast areas are threatened by fire and disease as the climate migrates out from under them, and persistent drought affects sections of all continents. People in those troubled lands look elsewhere for succor, leading to pressure on all frontiers, including the United States–Mexico border and the southern frontier of Europe.

The rate of climatic disruption is clearly set to rise abruptly over the next years and well into the next century. And the climatic disruption is but one of the trends triggered by growth. The trends, followed to the extreme, define a global environmental disaster that is economic and political as well, for a barren land has no economic base and nothing on which to build and sustain a government.

If the chaos of the post-Katrina New Orleans is not enough of a lesson, the island nation of Haiti on the western end of Hispaniola has all the elements of a model of the depths to which biotic impoverishment proceeds. Haiti is severely overpopulated and virtually totally deforested. Fisheries have yielded to overharvest and continued siltation from an eroding landscape. Agriculture has been driven to tiny plots on slopes as steep as thirty degrees that wash out in a year or so. Rivers flood regularly as rain in the mountains runs off immediately and follows new channels because older channels are filled with debris from the slopes. Settlements are flooded and people drown regularly in minor storms. No stable government has existed in Haiti for decades. Thuggery prevails. No stable government is possible until a stable and functional landscape can be restored to provide an economic base, a place to live, such essentials as a reliable supply of potable water and a sewage system. Government, economic vitality, and a functionally intact landscape depend on each other. Haiti is in an environmental, biophysical hole, an abyss, in fact. Outside financing will be required in the range of tens of billions of dollars to establish and execute a comprehensive plan for the restoration of a functional landscape, to relocate people, and to provide them with a way to make a living while the restoration proceeds, if restoration is to occur at all. An effective government, no matter the efforts, will await that restoration for its own emergence and success. Haiti is the victim of a progressively impoverished landscape to the point of environmental collapse. It matters not at all that the collapse was not specifically due to climatic disruption, which is but one factor among several that have the same effect—systematic, cumulative, biotic impoverishment, a cloud overhanging all of this civilization.

The costs of biotic impoverishment are with us now, but there is no one standing by on the moon, waiting to finance the restoration of Earth. Restoration is up to us. The world is travelling rapidly on a one-way street. The capitalist system, built to celebrate greed and a political system that feeds it, seems incompetent to respond by accepting the limits of growth and biophysical laws as global reality. Solutions, if they exist at all, will bubble up from below, be discovered by the public, and put into action, quite possibly without central governmental leadership. The problem is global, but "global" is the sum of local actions. Suddenly local and global biophysics touches us all, whether we recognize it or not. We are, each of us, and each place we occupy, an example for the world, a contributor to progressive impoverishment, or an increment of reform toward stability.

Science has a lot to say about "what works" in maintaining the human habitat. The ecologists' model of a functional world, an enduring human habitat, is well defined. It is the world that runs itself using the information contained in the genetic complement of the biota—all of it—for that is the only pool of information available and it cannot be replaced by any human hand. It is the product of millions of years of experiment in which the failures have fallen away and the successes are our inheritance. Our self-interest lies in respecting that inheritance, preserving it, and enabling it to function in maintaining the thin layer of the earth that we inhabit: the biosphere. And that is our business in science, not merely conservation, but the definition and redefinition of details of function as they apply to human activities. And, as the challenges to environmental stability grow, as they will in an ever tighter world, they become the core governmental purpose: keeping a habitat suitable for life, all life. Our job in science defines itself in this transition: what will work in the public interest and what will not?

Designing and building a house for a major institution involved in research and public policy on the environment at the beginning of the third millennium is no small challenge, but an obviously serious one. The Woods Hole Research Center provided the intellectual, administrative, and financial freedom to define and pursue new realms in ecology, all involved in defining and deflecting the general global slide into biotic impoverishment. Such comprehensive objectives require continuous review as opportunities close and other opportunities open. As the first decade of the new millennium advanced, it became abundantly clear that several biophysical issues were emerging powerfully enough as political issues to demand the full attention of science and government at all levels. They caught our attention, of course.

First, and most important, *the fossil fuel era must end* very rapidly with stabilization of the atmospheric burden by 2012 and subsequent reductions in emissions that reduce the atmospheric burden from nearly 400 parts per million (ppm) of carbon dioxide to 350 ppm in a short time, less than a decade, and to less within the ensuing years toward the approximately 300 ppm that existed at the beginning of the twentieth century.[5] (There are several additional steps to this transition. They include the end of coal, drastic reductions in the use of oil and gas, major global changes in the management of forests to preserve the remaining primary forests and to restore forests on 400,000–800,000 square miles of once-forested land.)

Second, a new perspective must arise, extending to the development and universal adoption of *a zero-release philosophy* to ensure that industrial and other pollutants, including agricultural chemicals, do not change the chemistry of the biosphere, even in small ways. The assumption that all chemicals except those that are directly hazardous to people in some conspicuous or well-defined way can be released safely is simply a fallacy. Worse, the assumption that the biota is immune to chemical disruption at low concentrations is also fallacious. The integrity of the chemistry of environment is essential to life.

Third, the new world will require a *new system for storing energy* and making it widely available to replace fossil fuels in a range of critical uses. Not discussed widely, but certainly well known, is the potential for the rapid development of a solar-based (including wind) hydrogen industry supported immediately by massive governmental subsidies with funds available from taxation of fossil fuels. The moment for that transition is now; the implications for the world are large and affect virtually all aspects of the human enterprise and its potential.

Fourth, the squeeze on energy is also a squeeze on food and on transportation. *Industrial agriculture is not capable of feeding the poor of the world,* who are not able to buy into it. The present system of moving massive quantities of food and other consumer goods great distances over land and by air is certain to break down as the price of fuel soars and demand also soars with growth in population and shifts in diet.

Fifth, although industrial agriculture will not collapse, *local agriculture will enjoy a rejuvenation* already underway, even in the industrialized countries. This transition is part of the energy revolution and will have ultimately profound effects on land use and land values as well as the distribution of dwellings. How large this transition will be is, of course, not known, but the pressures are building now as the energy/environment squeeze becomes more acute.

The first three of these issues were of immediate consequence in our planning. Agriculture was a less immediate concern. And we were not, of course, completely free agents in planning a new building and a campus. The Town of Falmouth, the Commonwealth of Massachusetts, and the Cape Cod Commission all had an interest and rules governing what we could do. But first, we had to decide just what we wanted in the context of what we saw as an appropriate example for the world, an example that reflected our view at the moment of the Great Issues. How far we would be able to go in establishing that example would probably depend on finances and regulations as well as imagination and common sense.

The fact is, however, that the issues are complicated and perspectives as to cause and effect differ with experience. Scientists steeped in climatology do not necessarily have a comprehensive understanding of the global metabolism of forests and soils and their potential for affecting the heat-trapping gas content of the atmosphere and thereby the climates of continents. And oceanographers are not necessarily either biologists or climatologists or especially interested in those fields. And once we look beyond science, the associations with global biophysics become even more tenuous. The compromises that lubricate politics and business often run roughshod over biophysical facts and laws, and scientists find themselves lonely voices in a political wilderness, begging for a chance to set some limits on compromises to keep them within the range of effectiveness. Meanwhile, politicians, challenged in their own domain, assert acidly that scientists do not set the rules for running the world and insist that "realistic compromises" must be made to preserve "the economy" and "our way of life," whatever the scientists say. It is the equivalent of the pilot of the large plane that has just lost power at 40,000 feet announcing in the silence as the plane gains momentum on its downward spiral that the passengers should not worry for he has just now rescinded the law of gravity and all will be well.

Similar challenges afflict conservation. Practitioners regularly assume that good intentions are enough to ensure progress. But good intentions uninformed by biophysical facts and laws are not only ineffectual but can be seriously misleading. The scale of the climatic disruption, for example, is grossly underestimated by many scientists and by virtually all politicians as a result of the very conservative approach that has marked the four technical reports issued by the Intergovernmental Panel on Climate Change. The Panel was established by the United Nations Environment Programme and the World Meteorological Organization to offer comprehensive reviews of the climatic disruption with data from the global scientific community. Four appraisals have been prepared, the latest in 2007.[6] The appraisals are conservative because the scientific community is reluctant to assert effects unless they are clearly defensible, and the community of scientists fully engaged in the issues is only a fraction of the larger community that is interested, has been consulted, and whose interests must be considered in the final report. Beyond that there is continuous pressure from economic and certain political interests to deny the need for, and to delay, any action in reducing the causes of the disruption of climate. The net effect is that the reports of the Intergovernmental Panel on Climate Change, as thoroughly detailed and accurate as they are, lag behind the changes in the world that are in fact moving more rapidly than most scientists, even the most experienced, anticipated. The misunderstanding, widely shared by politicians and many scientists and conservationists, presents a huge problem.[7]

Now we face in fact an urgent, immediate crisis that requires for resolution unified global action to manage forests and to reduce the use of fossil fuels almost immediately by twenty-five to fifty percent, more in a few years. The changes in management of forests are almost as demanding: the preservation of all remaining primary forests globally (a ban on harvests of all old-growth forests) and the reestablishment of forests on large areas of normally naturally forested land. Such an area, 300,000–700,000 square miles, of once forested land is the upper limit of what is available worldwide.[8] There is little room for compromise, if the action is to be effective. If not effective, the world moves inexorably down the scale of biotic impoverishment with endpoints defined by Haiti and a score of other similarly impoverished lands. Is that a reasonable compromise? Does the world realize that the compromise is being made and the changes are but the beginning of a slide that is bound to accelerate?

That perspective drove us in reflecting, not only on our business, but also on how we should proceed with our new campus. How would we address the Great Issues? There never was much question. Our business is environmental biophysics, ecology, how the world works, and how to keep it working in the long term as a suitable and wholesome habitat for people. Those issues start at home, and the early twentieth-century model of domestic independence characteristic of rural life in New England (and almost everywhere else) is a good start. That independence was shattered, of course, by the shift from local energy sources, which were in fact solar, to fossil fuels, which offered for a time a concentrated and portable and abundant source of energy. But fossil fuels, although abundant, never were infinitely available, but were industrially controlled and were an ineluctable source of pollution. Worse, the technology developed around them expanded the capacities of individuals for capturing and controlling other resources. Technology increased the demands of each individual on the environment. That expansion, compounded by an unprecedented surge in human numbers, has overwhelmed the earth. The conspicuous problem now is that we have far exceeded the capacity of the atmosphere to accommodate the waste products of fossil fuels, coal, oil, and gas. Worse, the cheap energy has allowed an expansion of human influences to the point where the major cycles of carbon, nitrogen, and other elements essential to life are affected and global climate is moving out from under life itself.

There is a new need for examination of our world, for a reappraisal of just how the world works, not only its political and economic systems, but also as a biophysical system. When the human influences were small in proportion to the earth as a whole, we could assume with some confidence that the global environment would restore any mistakes we made in local management of environmental affairs. That circumstance no longer prevails. We are changing the earth as a whole, introducing chronic global disruption of climate, of global chemistry, of all the biotic systems that maintain the human habitat. The environmental matrix that supports the human undertaking is at hazard and requires redefinition and reestablishment. So our job now is to restore a functional biosphere. That challenge starts at home, remaking the ways we live, not into the twentieth-century model, for that has passed, but into the postindustrial model in which the public interest is defined by, and focused on, keeping an environment that will support life indefinitely. Our emphasis was clear. We had been defining it for all of our lives and were facing at the moment the opportunity to design into our new campus as large a step as possible into the new world of renewable energy and closed industrial cycles that would respect and conserve the physical, chemical, and biotic integrity of the earth.

It is a scientific challenge of monstrous proportions, but it is our mission and the driving force behind the development of the Woods Hole Research Center and its new campus.

And Woods Hole, with its long history of scholarship in science, was clearly a fitting place for the excitement to begin.

2

BACK TO THE BEGINNING

The Woods Hole Research Center

I t was in one context a very bold and possibly foolish move, founding a new laboratory from nothing in pursuit of a unique set of objectives. In 1985 the Woods Hole Research Center was created from a well financed and successful institute of ecology, which I had myself started and built just ten years earlier under the umbrella of the Marine Biological Laboratory. I had had by that time, 1985, a great deal of experience, and not a little frustration, in building research programs in ecology. I had long thought that it was time for ecology to stand alone, to have its own intensively interested staff and trustees and supporters, and to be able to define its own objectives in a world that was badly in need of new principles of environmental science. And it was daily more important to move that knowledge into the business of government.

I had previously been at Brookhaven National Laboratory in a biology department that aspired to molecular biomedicine under an umbrella of high-energy physics and nuclear energy. Thinking about the environment was not specifically scorned, but it was assumed that everyone had mastered that topic long ago and there really was not much there to think about. Serious scholars in science pursued molecular biology or atom smashing. My view was that, despite the laboratory's history, the central purpose of Brookhaven National Laboratory was leadership in the emergent and demanding science of environment and I made no secret of that perspective. The physics community, busily engaged in the continuing competition for the largest particle accelerator in the world, did not, at least initially, universally share my mission, although they certainly did not discourage it and, ultimately, embraced it as the questions we asked and set about answering emerged.

There were interesting and revealing moments, many of them. Throughout the 1960s a small group of scientists around the world had been working on the global cycles of elements essential to life, especially carbon, but including nitrogen and sulfur, among others. It seemed especially appropriate for the program I had developed at Brookhaven to advance the then-emerging recognition of the importance of the buildup of carbon dioxide in the atmosphere. The laboratory supported the idea, and I arranged and financed a major symposium entitled "Carbon and the Biosphere" in 1972.[1] The world's leading scientists familiar with that topic—ecologists, oceanographers, climatologists, chemists—came to Brookhaven from as far away as Australia to discuss the great global cycles of carbon and sulfur and nitrogen and their importance in maintaining a habitable earth. The most we could gather on that topic from around the world was fifty scientists. As we completed our discussion of the fate of the earth and our guests packed to leave, participants in the next symposium gathered. The topic was a technical discussion of magnets, with special reference of course to the particle accelerators. Three hundred people gathered from around the world. We had a new and revealing perspective on the relative interest in the scientific community at that time on the fate of the earth versus magnetism.

As the Atomic Energy Commission was transformed in stages to the Department of Energy, money grew tighter at the national laboratories and missions drew new scrutiny and, occasionally, urgency in new directions. I had no interest in the development of reactors offshore on the continental shelves and even less interest in a new sea-level Isthmian Canal through Colombia to be excavated with nuclear charges. Nor had the unwise and ultimately ill-fated proposition that nuclear energy be used to excavate a new harbor at Cape Thompson on the northwest coast of Alaska appealed to me as worthy of much serious consideration. These were some of the topics open for consideration by environmental experts and others at the national laboratories. I had what I thought to be more fundamental interests.

Throughout all of these and many other discussions and throughout my whole tenure at Brookhaven I was treated very well. I discovered later that on occasion, without ever a word to me, I had been fiercely defended by the Brookhaven administration of that time from those troubled by my various activities in defining, for example, the persistence and hazards of DDT and other agricultural poisons.[2] I admired their steadfast support and their reticence in advertising it, a solid example of wisdom in management that was not lost. Despite the attractiveness of the national laboratory, after more than ten years of exciting work there, I decided that it was time to move on. I was by then sure that I would not under any circumstance enter the combat that was rending university biology departments where molecular biological interests were intolerant of all the rest of biology and especially unsympathetic to ecology. I had watched from nearby the ceaseless battles at Dartmouth, Harvard, and Yale, seen the sad migration of a group of distinguished ecologists from Yale to Dalhousie in Halifax, Canada, and wanted no part of such bootless contention.

When the opportunity arose, first, in discussions in 1972, to consider building a new institute of ecology at the Marine Biological Laboratory (MBL) in Woods Hole, there was not much question as to what to do. Over the next three years, with help from the MBL, I spent much time seeking support for the venture. At one point I found myself on an airplane headed for Washington, D.C., looking for a substantial grant from the National Science Foundation of one hundred thousand dollars or so to support the new institute. I found myself across the aisle from two good friends from Brookhaven, the director and another well known physicist, also bound for Washington on a similar mission. Their objective: a $30-million initial grant for planning a new accelerator, a sum that rivaled and may have exceeded all the money available for ecology in the National Science Foundation at that time. I wilted. Ecology and the fate of the earth clearly had a long way to go in this competition for attention and resources in science.

In 1975 the Marine Biological Laboratory, founded in 1888, was in its eighty-eighth year. It was making a difficult transition from operations restricted to summer courses to year-round operation. It was also at a nadir of financial success, virtually bankrupt, and the infusion of new vigor and money into a major effort of building an institute of ecology was not simply a timely intellectual leap, but also a pragmatic solution to near insolvency.

The initial step was the immediate establishment of a series of month-long special courses for undergraduates during the new January recess that the energy squeeze of the mid-1970s had produced in the nation's college and university system. The main course was ecology, a choice virtually dictated by the intensity of public interest in environmental issues that had generated the 1972 Stockholm Conference on the Human Environment. At almost the last minute the professor from Yale whom I had invited to teach the course ruled himself unavailable and I quickly arranged to give the course myself. It was in every way a delightfully rewarding time with a group of talented students and staff drawn from around the country. The course ran for several years after the founding of The Ecosystems Center, as we named the new venture, and gave rise to a new generation of distinguished scholars, some of whom took careers in science and are now emergent leaders. It was clear that a new era of environmental sciences had begun in the scientific community of Woods Hole as we accumulated staff and money and students and scholarly initiatives. And the courses we offered spread the word among students and the distinguished faculty who came from far and wide to no-holds-barred discussions of ecology. We had believers and nonbelievers, arguing it out before students.

I well recall the discussions with the distinguished geologist K. O. Emery, a member of the National Academy of Sciences, who had made a study of sea level around the world and argued that there was no credible evidence of recent increases then being discussed as linked to climatic warming and the melting of glacial ice. His reasoning was that the tipping of the continental plates obscured cause and effect and the differences due to climatic changes were too small to distinguish. Many of the students had never heard such discussions.

We pursued over the next years our long-term interest in the global carbon budget, especially in the heat-trapping gas content of the atmosphere and the vitally important role of forests. These interests moved with us as we established the Woods Hole Research Center as an independent entity in 1985.

We had been prime participants in establishing the scientific background for understanding what we had come to call *the global climatic disruption* that was then gaining momentum and recognition as a serious threat. The buildup of heat-trapping gases in the atmosphere and the inevitable consequences of that series of changes in the human habitat are at the core of life, biological in cause and effect, the beginning and potential end of human welfare. The responsibility of the scientific community never seemed clearer or more important, first to define the problem and then to solve it. Very few scientists had thought about the metabolism of the earth as a whole, the mass of carbon held in plants and soils, the relative importance of land and water in controlling the composition of the atmosphere. The oceanographers were well ahead with their analyses and thought they knew the net flow of carbon from an overburdened atmosphere into the giant oceanic carbon dioxide/carbonate/bicarbonate system.

Terrestrial scientists had only begun to think about the land and forests and their roles in affecting the composition of the atmosphere. The most important data were those of Charles David Keeling of the Scripps Institution of Oceanography in La Jolla, California, who had started in 1958 a record of the concentration of carbon dioxide in air sampled on the Scripps Pier and at 10,000 feet on Mauna Loa in the Hawaiian Islands. The record showed not only the annual increase in the concentration of carbon dioxide in the air the but also recorded at Mauna Loa an annual cycle with a peak concentration in April at the end of the northern winter and a minimum in September or October, the end of the northern summer. We had at Brookhaven, almost inadvertently through our efforts in measuring the metabolism of a forest, accumulated over years a parallel set of data on the atmosphere downwind of the continent. These data showed not only the upward trend, but also defined the annual cycle observed at Mauna Loa. The data taken at Brookhaven, however, in the center of Long Island sixty miles east of New York City, were clearly vulnerable to spikes of carbon dioxide from industrial and other sources. To reduce the effects of these large sources we averaged the minimum concentrations observed daily. These minima followed an annual course that was defined by the metabolism of the northern hemisphere, apparently dominated by the metabolism of forests. The amplitude of the change from late winter to late summer was more than three times the amplitude as measured at Mauna Loa in mid-Pacific. These data were being taken downwind of the North American forested zone, whose metabolism was large enough to change the composition of the atmosphere hemispherically by several percent in a few weeks!

The point we made then, more than forty years before the climatic crisis of the new millennium, was the importance of the metabolism of terrestrial vegetation, especially forests, in affecting, even controlling, the carbon dioxide content of the atmosphere. The metabolism of forests is the single most powerful influence on the composition of the atmosphere in the short term of weeks to months. The implications of this influence were profound for the world—and for a big segment of global environmental research over the next decades. The metabolism of forests is highly vulnerable to changes in climate and remains the second most important cause of, and potential cure for, the accumulation of carbon dioxide in the atmosphere. The most important factor, of course, remains the combustion of fossil fuels—coal, oil, and gas.

By 1985, when we moved to establish the Woods Hole Research Center, it was becoming clear that an international treaty was necessary and that details of the treaty must emerge from the scientific community. We were at the center of this discussion and free to proceed as we set forth with the new institution. We had both the insights in science and the opportunity to put the insights into action in government.

Kilaparti Ramakrishna, a specialist in international environmental law, through a quirk of good fortune, happened to be in Woods Hole and available for a year while his wife finished graduate work in Boston. Rama was an expert in the United Nations system, familiar with the scientific issues surrounding climatic change, familiar too with the development of international law, and interested in working with us. He joined our staff and over the next years managed to lead in the production of the 1992 Framework Convention on Climate Change, signed in Rio that year and ultimately ratified by more than 180 nations, including the United States.[3]

Suddenly, the issue of global climatic disruption emerged from subtleties of oceanography and environmental chemistry to a much more complex and threatening issue of global welfare involving the biosphere as a whole and its metabolism. And it had become a political issue of great consequence. The scientific community of Woods Hole, long focused on the issues of environment and unfettered by the mixed objectives of university responsibilities, had had a large role in defining the problem and clear responsibilities in resolving it.

WHY WOODS HOLE?

How did a small village on the south shore of Cape Cod become a diversified scientific and scholarly center? The answer lies in part in geography and in part in a succession of brilliant scholars who found unusual opportunities there.

Woods Hole is sheltered from the open sea by the peninsula of Cape Cod, the island to the south, Martha's Vineyard, and the Elizabeth Islands chain to the southwest (figure 2.1). The confluence of the inshore, southward-flowing Labrador Current, with its boreal flora and fauna, and the northeastward-flowing eddies of the Gulf Stream, with its austral influences, has made the region rich in marine resources. The low-lying glacial

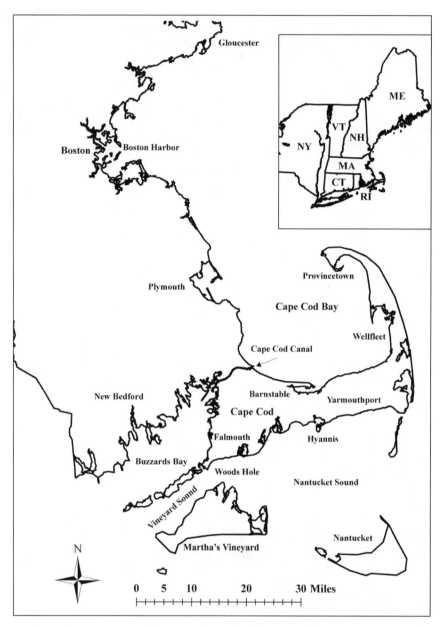

Figure 2.1   Eastern Massachusetts and Cape Cod.

outwash provides abundant sandy beaches and tidal shoals that have appealed to all generations from the very first inhabitants of postglacial time. Eastward lies one of the most productive fisheries in the world, Georges Bank, which was, 10,000 years ago, before the big glacial melt, dry land. "Woods Hole" is the passage between the end of the southwestern promontory of Cape Cod and the northernmost of the Elizabeth Islands, which are part of the same glacial moraine. Although it is not entirely clear to the non-sailor why the passages between these islands were called "holes," to a sailor they almost name themselves. The passages are narrow and rocky. Strong tidal currents make them dangerous even in these days of highly powered boats. The passages were especially dangerous in the days of sail when the strong tidal currents could easily carry a boat moving on a light wind onto the rocks. The major tidal passages between the islands of the Elizabeth chain were all blessed as holes—Woods Hole, the northernmost; Robinsons Hole; and Quicks Hole, the widest and safest.[4]

Sheltered from the open sea, the area has always attracted the curious, including the early indigenous Algonquin bands and, much later, English settlers who built scholarly enterprises around themselves.

The village at the end of the peninsula was of course named for the adjacent channel. Today Woods Hole is an informally defined section of the town of Falmouth, Massachusetts. The section of the town just north of the village of Woods Hole is Quissett, another informally defined area around Quissett Harbor. The Ordway Campus (the building we are discussing here) is in Quissett.

Woods Hole and Quissett form the southern tip of the peninsula, which is a southwest-trending glacial moraine that extends as far as Fishers Island on the Connecticut shore. Eastward of the peninsula are Vineyard and Nantucket sounds; westward, Buzzards Bay.

The eight acres in the original purchase by the Center is a section of the ridge that is the highest point on the peninsula there, about 2.5 miles north of the very tip of the peninsula.

The region was largely forested at the time of the first European settlement in the early 1600s, but the forest was the diminutive pitch pine-

sprout oak forest on the uplands with pockets of oak-chestnut and occa-
sional white pines and beeches in protected areas. Fire, almost certainly
regularly set by the Wampanoag residents to keep the landscape open, was
the dominant influence on the landscape and had been for centuries. The
burning ensured the persistence of the open, fire-resistant pitch pine–oak
forest on the upland moraines and outwash plains of Cape Cod. The chestnut (*Castanea dentata*) disappeared, the victim of an exotic fungus now en-
demic in the North American *Fagaceae*, the large beech family that includes
the oaks (*Quercus*) as well as the chestnut. The fungus was imported and
spread rapidly during the early decades of the twentieth century, leaving
the impoverished, fire-resistant pine-oak forest as the upland vegetation of
the glacial landscape.

At the time of European settlement in the very early years of the seven-
teenth century, corn (maize), beans, and cucurbits were being cultivated in
coastal regions of New England, including nearby on the Elizabeth Islands,
but the native populations had been devastated by European diseases, as
described for most of the Americas by Mann[5] and for New England earlier
by several authors. The plague of 1616–1620, probably smallpox, brought
destruction to indigenous populations at a rate of ninety percent, possibly
higher in some areas, and left cultivated fields abandoned to be taken up
by the European settlers, including the Plymouth settlement of 1620. The
region was rich in resources that had been exploited by the Wampanoag.
The extraordinary abundance of inshore populations of cod, together with
shellfish and the early stages of agriculture, provided an apparently inex-
haustible supply of food but did not prevent the trials of the settlers of Plymouth Colony, which began with their arrival on these shores late in the
last year of that devastating plague.

That colony, although much reduced by hardships in that first winter,
survived, with many others east and west along the coast, and exploited
the sea and the land with vigor. Virtually all of the land was pastured over
the next three centuries, and pictures of Woods Hole as late as the early
decades of the twentieth century show an open landscape almost devoid of
trees (figure 2.2).

Figure 2.2 Cumloden in about 1870, looking eastward from Treetops, across the road from the site of Hilltop House, not then constructed. The landscape, originally forested, had been stripped of trees for firewood and lumber and grazed for more than 150 years. The demand for firewood was virtually insatiable in those years, and there were literally no forests remaining. (Photo courtesy of the Woods Hole Historical Society)

Science and scholarship and efforts at conservation of natural resources came inevitably into this history. In 1870 (figure 2.3) the young Spencer Fullerton Baird, Assistant Secretary of the Smithsonian Institution under Joseph Henry and an avid student of fish and fisheries, was drawn to the richness of the regional fauna with its mixture of northern and southern waters. He collected extensively and found wherever he went concern about the "rapid decrease in the productivity of the fisheries."[6] Baird wrote in 1871 in a letter to the Committee on Appropriations of the U.S. Congress: "The belief is everywhere loudly expressed that unless some remedy be applied—whatever that may be—the time is not far distant when we shall lose, almost entirely, this source of subsistence and support, a calamity

Figure 2.3 Woods Hole in about 1870. The Eel Pond is in the left foreground with the Candle House, now the administrative center for the Marine Biological Laboratory, and Great Harbor beyond. The large buildings to the right are those of the "guano factory." The water in the background beyond Great Harbor is Woods Hole, the channel connecting Vineyard Sound and Buzzards Bay. The new laboratory, the MBL, was established in 1888 on the western end of the Eel Pond. (Photo courtesy of the Woods Hole Historical Society)

which would involve a vast number of evils in its train." The Congress appointed him to a new unpaid position as Commissioner of Fish and Fisheries. Baird established the work of the commission in temporary quarters on Little Harbor in Woods Hole in summer 1871. Later, in 1885, new quarters were constructed on Great Harbor on land purchased from Isaiah Spindle for $7,250. An additional gift of land from Joseph Story Fay was received adjacent to the Spindle land and extending along the waterfront to the then guano factory on Great Harbor. Baird sought support from others for this laboratory in pursuit of his continuing interests in teaching and research. The facilities were open to visiting scholars from around the world who came, especially in the summer, to study and teach.[7]

In 1872, more than 250 years after the Plymouth settlement, the Swiss zoologist Louis Agassiz, then a professor at Harvard and late in his brilliant scientific career, sought an opportunity to teach a summer course in marine biology. He advertised the course and sought support for it from the Massachusetts legislature. His public efforts drew the attention of a merchant in New York, John Anderson, who offered the island of Penikese near the western end of the Elizabeth Islands chain southwest of Woods Hole as the site for the course. Anderson ultimately provided $50,000 to build the Anderson School of Natural History on the site, which opened in 1873 with forty-three students carefully chosen by Agassiz from "hundreds" of applicants.[8] That was the beginning of a formal academic interest in science in the area, and the class he drew together was remarkable. Not surprisingly, perhaps, several of its young members, originally attracted by the well-known Agassiz, who had sorted out details of the glacially carved landscape, also became distinguished scientists over the next years. One, Charles Otis Whitman, became the first director of the Marine Biological Laboratory when it was founded in Woods Hole fifteen years later.

Louis Agassiz died in December 1873 and the school was run by his son, Alexander, during the following summer. Interest waned, however, and the difficulties in reaching the island by boat from Woods Hole proved too great, and the school was never run again. The elaborate school buildings burned in 1891 after many efforts at restoring the school had failed.[9]

In those same years beginning in 1871, according to the chronicle of Lillie (1944), the Woman's Education Association of Boston and the Boston Society of Natural History opened a field laboratory in Annisquam, Massachusetts, for the training of young biologists. By 1886 the Woman's Education Association in a meeting with biologists decided that it was time to establish a permanent laboratory and voted to seek $15,000 to support it for five years, appointed a board of trustees, and "proceeded to solicit subscriptions."

It was 1888 when the Women's Education Association coalesced with local interest in Woods Hole to found the Marine Biological Laboratory. The new institution was to expand its educational mission by offering summer courses open to all taught by scientists from around the country. The objective was to open the possibility for a summer curriculum in marine biology in the field, and courses were offered on marine algae and invertebrate zoology and later in ecology. It was a thoroughly democratic institution run by the scientists themselves. It was an academic distinction to be engaged as professor or student in summers at Woods Hole, and many lifelong personal and professional associations emerged spanning generations.

The MBL, as the laboratory was soon dubbed, benefited from the surge in interest in the expansion of science in the latter part of the nineteenth century. That interest had deep roots in the midcentury publications of Darwin and Wallace on evolution and George Perkins Marsh's 1864 book on natural history and human interests.[10] New England was ready for the vigor of the Agassiz dynasty and the energy and persistence of Spencer Baird, who had taken over as Secretary of the Smithsonian Institution after Secretary Joseph Henry's death in 1878. The laboratory that Baird had established at Woods Hole even before the Anderson School is now the National Marine Fisheries Service Laboratory operated under the National Oceanic and Atmospheric Administration of the U.S. Department of Commerce. It retains its focus on the fisheries of the northwest Atlantic.

These were the beginnings of Woods Hole as a scientific center. First was the personal interest in fish and fisheries of the young Spencer Baird, whose interests extended in time to preserving the richness of the fisheries and encouraging research and education generally. His activities were soon complemented by the vigor and insights of Louis Agassiz and his son, Alexander, and their efforts through the Anderson School of Natural History. The regional interests followed in establishing the MBL. The two laboratories thrived, one as a governmental laboratory, the other as a private summer institution open to scholars who found an unusual opportunity in Woods Hole to do research and teach marine biology. By 1930, as a result of discussions and study at the National Academy of Sciences, established only two decades earlier than the MBL to advise the government on needs in the development of science, there was an understandable interest in expanding knowledge of the oceans globally. It seemed wise to have an

East Coast center of oceanography quite apart from the specific studies of fisheries and coastal biology. This new oceanographic effort was to complement the West Coast's Scripps Institution of Oceanography in La Jolla. A group at the MBL sought to establish a year-round presence in the institution to pursue such studies. The trustees of the MBL did not wish to see the identity of the institution they had established diluted or changed, or to have to compete for space and other institutional resources with a year-round program, and, although blessing this group, encouraged them to establish themselves independently. The Woods Hole Oceanographic Institution was founded in 1930 with substantial help from the MBL and others. It acquired its ketch, the *Atlantis,* still famous around the world for its pioneering oceanographic cruises, although the ship was long ago sent into retirement in Argentina.

I remember well the *Atlantis*, although I never sailed on her. I was, I guess, ten years old, when father took me on a trip from Boston, where we lived then, to visit Woods Hole. The *Atlantis* was in, and father, himself a sailor brought up on the coast of Maine and a veteran of the seagoing navy in World War I, was drawn to her. The captain at that time was aboard and showed us the ship, including his cabin, where he and father talked at length while I stood in awe of the whole. Years later I met the *Atlantis* again. By then I was a young naval officer myself, aboard a small diesel oceanographic survey ship. We passed the *Atlantis* close aboard in the Straits of Florida on a magnificent day and I stood in awe again, this time of those young scientists whose highly constructive jobs took them to sea in warm waters on that sturdy, businesslike ketch.

The oceanographic institution thrived and expanded greatly during World War II and subsequently. It has over the past half century dominated the scientific community of the village, which now has additional scholarly institutions, including a second highly mature and professional national laboratory of the U.S. Geological Survey, with a spirited new group of environmental scientists.

The MBL ultimately developed a limited year-round presence in research with a program in ecology and systematics. The idea of year-round operation was not new but the first program was late in coming and somewhat limited in perspective. It provided the basis for acquiring a substantial, steel-hulled, diesel-powered research vessel, the *A. E. Verrill,* which was used by many scholars from around the world to inventory the marine life of the shallow waters of the region. A new approach was initiated in 1972 when I was asked to join the MBL and seek money to build a year-round institute of ecology. The Ecosystems Center was founded in 1975 and continues today in its own buildings on the MBL campus in the village.

Much had changed in science since the MBL was founded. Although students and staff were still interested in learning invertebrate zoology and classification of algae and in pursuing descriptive studies of ecology, there had been explosive growth of knowledge in biochemistry and physiology and neurobiology, and the curricula of the MBL were transformed. More than that, there had been major advances in ecology marked by discovery that human activities were changing the chemistry of the whole earth and had the potential to seriously threaten human health and welfare. These advances came following the extensive tests of nuclear weapons in Nevada and in the South Pacific in the early 1950s. The biological sciences were in a new and exciting and very important phase, literally emerging as the core of essential knowledge for the next century. Meanwhile, the MBL was in financial straits, locked into its summer program model and unable to raise the money needed to survive as an institution.

The financial problem was not new. It had risen in the early years as Charles Otis Whitman realized both the potential of the laboratory and the requirements for financial and institutional success. His recommendations, based on ten years of experience, and elaborate parallel initiatives by others interested in providing a broader financial base, were scorned by trustees devoted to the sanctity of the summer courses led by university-based experts from around the world. Whitman's enthusiasm dimmed and the laboratory struggled on, tied to the original model of summer operation supplementing university programs and suffering the financial consequences. All came to a head again in the 1970s when the transitions in science and financing forced a reappraisal.

In 1972 the MBL trustees, pushed by continuing financial emergency and by the evolution of science itself, agreed to a major new venture in full-time research. The trustees of that time, to their credit, recognized the tectonic upheavals that had already moved science far from the descriptive field studies that had been the early interest of staff and students at the MBL. Biology was fissured between a surging interest in biochemistry and medicine and a parallel surge in ecology and environment. The global circulation of the radionuclides produced by tests of nuclear weapons proved to be a model for the circulation of industrial toxins such as DDT and other persistent poisons. Worse, these substances were being picked up in living systems where they might be concentrated to levels that were acutely toxic. Suddenly we had discovered that every human on earth carried a burden of radioactivity from the bomb tests and a burden of DDT residues from the almost ubiquitous use of DDT, a very long-lived insecticide. After an extensive formal review completed in 1972, William Ruckelshaus, then administrator of the U.S. Environmental Protection Agency, substantially banned DDT for use in the United States. Tests of nuclear weapons had previously been driven underground to avoid further global contamination. It was a new world that required new ventures in science.

Dr. James D. Ebert, a distinguished embryologist and active member of the National Academy of Sciences, was the part-time director of the MBL. Ebert had come to me at Brookhaven to explore my interest. Ebert was a powerful supporter, and it was his wisdom and vigor that had led the trustees into the new venture. Three years later, in 1975, we had accumulated enough money to make a formal move, hire staff, and begin operation in Woods Hole.

It became clear during this period that the laboratory had to move toward a full-time director within a very few years and Ebert was the obvious choice, an excellent one. Ebert, however, was not long for that office; he was soon asked to become the president of the Carnegie Institution of Washington, an invitation that he could not refuse and one that ruled out his continued leadership of the MBL. Ebert's departure opened a difficult period for the MBL. The very success of The Ecosystems Center in developing programs and attracting money made it a target for those interested in supporting other objectives less well financed. This conflict set the stage for the move to start a new, independent institution with its own board of trustees devoted to the great issues of ecology and the global environment.

The trustees of the MBL, drawn largely from the academic biomedical users of the Laboratory, settled, not surprisingly, on one of their own, Dr. Paul Gross, then at the University of Rochester, as full-time director. The Ecosystems Center was at that time the only year-round activity of the Laboratory, and it accounted for a major fraction of the Laboratory's total budget. Although I had no personal interest in taking the position of director, I did have a vital interest in ensuring that the experience and perspectives of the new leadership would incorporate the Center's ambitious program, which depended entirely on its ability to raise money. The Center had been, and remained, a major contributor to the restoration of the Laboratory's financial security. The appointment, however, was made *ex cathedra,* almost in secret, with no consultation with our staff or with me, despite the earlier commitments when The Ecosystems Center was established.

Gross inherited a difficult challenge in transforming the Laboratory from its famous role as a summer institution to a new role as a year-round center of research and education in both biomedicine and environment. It was a contentious time. Many efforts arose to deflect the use of the grants accumulated to support ecology into various aspects of biomedicine that were asserted to be "environmental." The trustees, many not at all interested in The Ecosystems Center's program, did not cover themselves with glory as the arguments boiled.

The futile, wasteful struggles within the MBL continued, as did the competition within academic biology between biomedical interests and ecology. Again, I wanted none of it and admired instead the successful models of such conservation agencies as the World Wildlife Fund, the Natural Resources Defense Council, the Environmental Defense Fund, and The Conservation Foundation.

In the late 1960s and early 1970s, with colleagues in science and conservation, I had become engaged in founding these conservation law groups, especially the Environmental Defense Fund on Long Island and, a few years later, the Natural Resources Defense Council in New York. The mission of these groups was, as far as I was concerned, centered on forcing the government to obey its own laws and do its job of using the insights of science to protect the public interest in a wholesome and safe and enduring human habitat. That mission required far more detailed insight into the workings of the world, the mission of science with ecology at the core. Our objectives were defining themselves: they had become not only to determine how the world works, but also how to keep it working. It was a big step in science.

It had long been clear that such institutions had programs that floated on a core of scientific information. The connection with science was remote, however, even ephemeral. My vision had been that the World Resources Institute, founded by Gus Speth with a major grant from the McArthur Foundation in 1982, would offer that connection. It did, in fact, but not through a new scientific venture as I had dreamed, only through a much closer scholarly connection to the scientific community. There was much new analysis by brilliant scholars, but no new research. I saw a continuing, even intensified, need for a freestanding scientific institution with its own board of trustees focused in science on the great issues of environment.

More than that, environmental issues had become larger and more threatening, even acute, and the new Republican administration under Reagan actively scorned them. The attitude was defined immediately as the new administration accumulated and destroyed the comprehensive final report of the president's Council on Environmental Quality (CEQ), the *Global 2000 Report,* produced under President Carter by Gus Speth, chair of the CEQ. The report dealt intensively with the climatic disruption, an emphasis that I, as a long-term friend and admirer of Speth, had supported with articles and widely cited testimony[11] and had otherwise encouraged at that time in every way. Reagan gave the country a further sign of scorn for environmental issues by cutting the budget of the CEQ and environmental programs in other governmental agencies.

The enduring need for continued, nongovernmental environmental research in the public interest could not have been more clearly enunciated. That research was our business, and I was increasingly interested in moving out from under the MBL umbrella with all its meddling and controversy and narrow focus on university interests as opposed to what we considered the emergent Great Issues involving the expansion of human influences globally and the accelerating erosion of the only human habitat available.

The scale of the human activities had reached phenomenal proportions, a major geological transformation moving carbon stored in the earth's crust over hundreds of millions of years into the atmosphere as carbon dioxide, all in a period of less than two centuries. At the same time we had transformed the face of the earth from about forty-four percent forested land to less than twenty-eight percent forested. The transformations continue today with implications for the global energy and water balances and changes in climate as the earth continues to warm.[12] A parallel, related, and no less threatening series of problems exists from progressive biotic impoverishment, from rapidly accumulating toxification as the chemistry of air, water, and land is changed, and from the continued expansion of the human population into an eroding environment.

Gross and then chairman of the trustees of the MBL, Prosser Gifford, made it very clear that these topics were not to be pursued energetically under the MBL's aegis, at least by me. The primary institutional interests were in cultivating biomedicine in all of its ramifications. Ecology might be tolerated, but in my eyes it needed the full support of a board of trustees and the ability to reach into public affairs, as seemed increasingly necessary and appropriate. We were, after all, firsthand observers of a series of transitions in the earth that have major implications for human welfare. The opportunity at the MBL had passed, and it was time to move on.

The experience that led me to this new, personal departure in science included fourteen exciting years of research in ecology at Brookhaven National Laboratory on Long Island and more than ten years building The Ecosystems Center, as well as close associations with academic departments at Yale, Dartmouth, Duke, and Harvard, among others. The experience extended to watching the development of the Ecological Society's Institute of Ecology, which suffered and ultimately foundered on the same shoals of ego and jealousy and competition that had burdened the MBL more or less continuously from its very early years. Meanwhile, the world was sliding rapidly into the pattern of conspicuous biotic impoverishment that we had identified so definitively in the research at Brookhaven as the product of chronic exposure to ionizing radiation and, in fact, any chronic disturbance.[13] Those insights continued to play a large role in the revolution in conservation in the late 1960s and early 1970s as conservation passed a major transition into public affairs.

The Woods Hole Research Center emerged over the next years as a major force in research to inform policy responses to a series of global environmental issues, chief among them the potential for the climatic disruption as the trigger for the collapse of this civilization.

Nothing was simple, but there was broad understanding of the importance of having a freestanding research institution devoted to global biophysics in a world that was burdened with a still rapidly expanding human population and a climatic disruption of ill-defined consequence. The field of ecology was to be expanded and the information, insights, and principles developed would be essential elements in gauging the seriousness of the changes in climate already entrained. The timing was appropriate and the scientific center of Woods Hole, with its century and a quarter of emphasis on science and environment, was the place.

The combined activities of five vigorous scholarly institutions in Woods Hole had spread the name and reputation of the village as a scientific center worldwide. As our activities expanded and we sought new space in Woods Hole, we found ourselves in competition with the other institutions, also growing, and with a vigorous summer colony. One of the older buildings in the village, a bed and breakfast, at the head of Little Harbor close to the site of the original settlement became available. We purchased

Figure 2.4 Davis House at the head of Little Harbor in Woods Hole in about 1988 when it was a bed and breakfast inn. It originally had a central chimney and a fireplace in every room. The central chimney had been removed and replaced by a central staircase many years prior to our purchase. The building is landmark, constructed in 1804, close to the site of the original settlement at the head of Little Harbor. It had housed many distinguished visitors, including Spencer Baird while he was establishing the original Fisheries Commission and early courses in science in Woods Hole. We removed the unheated porch and refurbished the building inside and out for its new purposes. (By permission, Dana Gaines, Martha's Vineyard)

it in 1989 and named it Davis House (figure 2.4) for its first owner. It had been built in about 1804 and required extensive renovation for the Center's use. It was constructed simply and inexpensively using timbers and sheathing from other buildings, possibly in part from the locally famous guano fertilizer factory on Great Harbor in Woods Hole that had failed in that period. The back wall of the main part of the building was constructed of a single layer of heavy, used, sawn planks laid vertically against a simple frame for two stories, shingled outside and plastered inside. This simple plank wall can still be seen in the back stairway.

An imaginative plan for expanding Davis House proved inadequate, and adjacent buildings and land were not available. We leased what we could in the village. Ultimately we occupied part or all of five separate buildings in Woods Hole, all linked with telephone and computer cables, although removed from one another. And we required still more space. Consolidation of activities in one place became an increasingly urgent need.

Meanwhile, with the ownership and renovation of Davis House, our newly invented logo displayed prominently on a sign on the main road in the village, and the experience of the summer courses at the MBL behind us, we and ecology had become firmly established in the tight scholarly village dominated by an annual cycle of science. But it was not long before the community was shaken by the prospect of losing its famous Woods Hole address.

The building housing the post office was being put up for sale and the post office was to be moved to Falmouth. The possibility caught wide attention. There had long been competition among residents, year-round and summer, to have a low-numbered Woods Hole post office box, or even any box at all in Woods Hole. Suddenly, a century and a quarter of identity of families and institutions and science and scholarship with the village of Woods Hole seemed to be coming to an ignoble end with a new address in Falmouth. The thought brought public outrage.

The bank in the village that owned the post office found it to be a distraction. The Woods Hole Post Office, a substation of the Falmouth office, could not buy the building, and Woods Hole was to lose its local office. The community quickly rallied around the challenge and, through the Woods Hole Community Foundation under the leadership of one of the Center's trustees, bought the building from the bank and saved the post office. The community now owns the building and rents it to the post office.

In the ensuing weeks the community made T-shirts printed with the Woods Hole postal mark and sold them on the street in the village to a grateful public. As the market was saturated and the sales diminished, the stamp was changed and the market was rejuvenated. The world famous saga of science in Woods Hole, embedded in a century and a quarter of history, in the literature of science, and in the memories of thousands, continues with its Woods Hole address.

By the late 1990s expansion of the Center's program brought intensive systematic efforts to find and purchase expanded quarters for the Center in the village. As the efforts proved futile, because the village was "full," the staff and trustees sought alternatives that might allow the construction of a new building appropriate for the special needs of research in ecology. The needs included office space, meeting rooms, auditorium for seminars, a wet laboratory, large open rooms for the maps and charts used in remote sensing of global features, as well as abundant space for elaborate computer support. Managing energy was a major consideration, troubled as we were by the lack of interest in the MBL leadership over previous years in building even to conserve energy. And the issues of water and wastes, especially toxins, were, of course, high on our list of interests. The purchase of Hilltop House in Quissett came as the culmination of several years of searching within the village of Woods Hole for an appropriate site for a campus of this small but expanding young scholarly institution. We had found sites and had made attractive offers, but no deal had emerged. Real estate prices had run away from all and trustees were impatient. Our director of development led us to Hilltop, and I, as the director, reluctant beyond reason to leave the village, finally came with others for a look. The big old house was in disrepair, buried in overgrown woody plantings, long neglected, that shaded a rotting porch that had been abandoned on one side of the house and was close to collapsing elsewhere. My immediate response, recorded for posterity by our staff and later brought gleefully to life, was *never.* But where else could we find eight acres? I walked the perimeter and had another look at the house. For a price, we might make something of it. We could follow the Oceanographic Institution and the Sea Education Association and leave the village. And there really was no alternative, whatever our wishes. The price of the "three-million-dollar" four-acre estate on the water close to the village that we had thought we had purchased earlier at the price named by the owner had jumped to six million, and we had moved on. Hilltop House became the only real possibility, and the director's *never* became *now or never,* and we hastened this time to follow our director of development's persistent and sound advice.

Hilltop House was a Victorian mansion, at one time used as a hotel on the outskirts of Woods Hole overlooking the southern coast of Cape Cod. In recent years it had been a summer house for the Rev-Kury family. The family had come as refugees from the persecutions of World War II and had prospered here with careers in medicine and with the operation of a fine restaurant, The Café Budapest in Boston. (I have always wondered whether that handsome fungus ever made its way to the menu.)

When the family, diminished by the death of Livia's sister and still busy in medicine as well as with running a popular restaurant, decided to sell their summerhouse, they held a giant yard sale of the furnishings of the mansion. It was a difficult moment for owners who were leaving a favorite summer refuge and parting with long-familiar things. It was a feast for the visitors and a fascinating moment in history for the purchasers of one of the most spectacular sites on the road between the Falmouth Green and the village of Woods Hole.

We, the scientists and staff and trustees and friends of the Woods Hole Research Center, were excited and pleased to look forward to a new campus, a single new building, albeit somewhat removed from our institutional roots in the village. The yard sale was a big event with food and an auction and scores of visitors, all on the two-acre lawn in front of the famous mansion, now in disrepair. Curiosity rather than need dominated, and the curious had much to explore. It was also cathartic, a housecleaning to make way for the new, broader purposes we had in mind.

That day was the first in the transition of the eight-acre tract and the 1877 mansion into the Gilman Ordway Campus of the Woods Hole Research Center, then in its fifteenth year. The Ordway Campus offered the opportunity not only to consolidate scientific activities, but also to be a continuing example of the principles we develop and advance in both science and public affairs. It was the first step on a road that was much longer and more tortuous than anyone at that stage could, or might wish to, imagine. The trip was exciting, informative, funny, sad, and instructive, even exhilarating, in varying degrees all along the way.

As we took possession of our soon-to-be campus, we enjoyed a surge of enthusiastic anticipation, not only of the still long-off move into new quarters after fifteen years of struggling with jury-rigged facilities, but also in anticipation of a much enhanced capacity to build the Center's program around the great issues of environment that were exploding onto the global stage. We, the youngest of the five scientific institutions in Woods Hole, had worked very effectively in defining our special role as a privately financed nongovernmental scientific institution with a special commitment to environmental interests in the public realm. We were especially sensitive and defensive of our objectivity in defining and defending the public interest as opposed to various private or commercial interests. That sensitivity extended to financing of our work. We could not, for instance, have Exxon or Texaco on our masthead as a donor if we wished to be taken seriously in our elaborations of details of the climatic disruption, a major program of the Center. Even the appearance of a conflict of interests was to be avoided. We had, fifteen years previously, separated ourselves from the Marine Biological Laboratory to escape the pressures and conflicts of the larger institution with far broader objectives that regularly brought, or sought to bring, awkward compromises in objectives our way.

There were many factors governing the analyses that followed. The first, of course, were the site, the existing house and land, and their history. Second was the overarching purpose of the institution as scientists and scholars looked toward the next century and the inevitable clash of human numbers and aspirations with the limits of the earth. Any construction had to be consistent with our vision as to what is appropriate for the buildings of the beginning of the new millennium. Our building should stand as a model for the decades in which the global environment emerges as The Great Issue, displacing economic and political competition with an essential new focus on preserving the biosphere as human habitat. That perspective was universally endorsed by our staff and trustees and governed all decisions. We could draw on the experience of David Orr and colleagues at Oberlin College where they had, with great difficulty, broken the mold of reactionary conservatism in campus construction, at least for a moment, and built a solar-powered building surrounded by a model landscape on the somewhat limited campus of the college. It was, to be sure, an uphill fight to persuade a fundamentally conservative college administration that in this new world, bold new departures in architectural purpose and design are necessary.

We had greater freedom than Oberlin could offer, much more land, and none of the constraints of an existing urban campus. The site was on the main road north of the village. It was within easy reach of the bicycle path constructed on the old railway bed between Falmouth Center and Woods Hole. From the standpoint of the staff, it was centrally located. Most lived outside the village, several in Falmouth nearby, so travel was reduced and the possibility of using the bicycle path was real enough. We had, moreover, an existing building set comfortably on the highest land at that point of the peninsula, so there was no question as to where and what we would build. We could take advantage of the rapidly accumulating experience of leaders in both design and construction. The central issues as we saw them had much to do with energy, of course, but these energy issues reached into the details of construction, insulation, materials used in construction, and the flow of water in the completed building.

Although we had all been attracted by Bill McDonough, making the final selection of the architect was not easy. McDonough, then the dean of the School of Architecture at the University of Virginia in Charlottesville, had a reputation for imaginative approaches and several spectacular nationally recognized successes, including the turf-topped Gap headquarters in San Bruno, California, and the new environmental center at

Oberlin. He was another admirer of Marc Rosenbaum, the engineer we knew and later hired who had made a business of consulting on energy efficiency in architecture.

I sought David Orr's advice and ultimately visited his new building on the Oberlin campus. It was clear that Bill McDonough had responded to that opportunity sensitively and well. There were critics at Oberlin who scorned the solar energy, the John Todd sewage treatment system that became an integral educational part of the building,[14] and the message that David Orr had brought to the campus. But such critics exist everywhere and often perform a useful role in drawing forth far more powerful data and arguments than would have come forth without the criticism. So it was at Oberlin, and the educational mission was clear and powerfully advanced at every turn. Orr agreed to be an advisor for our effort and was a critical, but effective, supporter of Bill McDonough.

Bob Fisher, a friend of long standing, and one of the owners of The Gap, was proud of their new McDonough-designed building in San Bruno, just south of San Francisco and adjacent to the San Francisco airport. I took myself on a brief tour of that magnificent building with its living roof.

Wandering through the generously open space of a handsome headquarters building, I had to be impressed with the energy and activity of the dwellers but was quickly persuaded that, attractive and appropriate as the building was for Gap, it was testimony to the imagination and versatility of the architects but not a model I could take back to a skeptical trustee of a fundamentally conservative academic enterprise.

McDonough's imagination and experience at Oberlin and his conspicuous versatility captured us and we decided to work with him, persuaded as we were that he would not only meet our expectations in design but would also help in the search for funds, always a consideration in any such project. We were at that point pleased to imagine a new and promising chapter in the history of the site, the region, and the saga of science in Woods Hole.

Our previous institutional experience in both design and construction, supplemented by advice from the Oberlin experience, put the ultimate responsibility for design and supervision squarely on the institution, its leadership, trustees, and staff. We were blessed in that we had a board whose members were completely behind the project in every way. More than that, we had a staff that was enthusiastic and knowledgeable and relentless in its analyses and, later, in scrutiny of plans. The board's leadership extended to enthusiastic and imaginative engagement in fusing the mission of the institution and the new campus into a vision for the new millennium. How far could we go in advancing such dreams?

3

REDESIGNING HILLTOP HOUSE

Triumphs and Compromises

There were several practical matters that required special consideration immediately as initial steps in considering the design of new construction. There was the Victorian mansion of Hilltop House and the extent to which it might be used, the siting of a new building on our new tract, the heating system, the water supply, the sewage treatment issue, the contours of the land, and the questions surrounding energy supply and uses, not to speak of the landscaping, the forest land (figure 3.1), and the interests of neighbors.

Our objectives were the picture of conservatism: low energy consumption and, ideally, having remaining energy needs met by renewable energy sources; an emphasis on local materials, with a preference for construction with wood that had been locally milled and grown in forests managed for long-term production; no toxic materials; no plastics that would not decay when the useful life of the building had passed. We wanted a well insulated building with double- or triple-glazed windows that would be tight in New England's winter winds and would have low emissivity and limited losses to radiant heat. We envisioned a building well lighted with natural light and comfortable in all seasons. These requirements were to be applied to an approximately 20,000-square-foot building and seemed to demand that

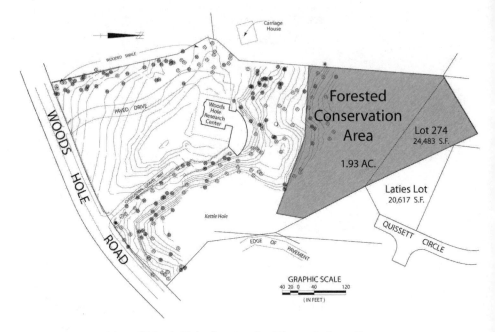

Figure 3.1   Map of Woods Hole showing the Gilman Ordway Campus.

the surface-to-volume ratio be as low as possible simply to conserve resources in construction and energy in operation. (We ruled out a sphere,
however efficient, as impractical.) The only practical approach, if the existing building were to be used in whole or in part, was a new wing attached
to the existing building and following the contours of the hill in a gentle
curve to the northeast (figure 3.1). This chapter describes the considerations that went into that decision.

THINKING ABOUT ENERGY

Energy drew much attention, for we had to abandon fossil fuels and, if possible, arrange for no combustion at all on-site, yet the building would un-

questionably require heat in winter and, quite probably, cooling in summer. At the same time we wanted to produce our own electricity on-site and, if possible, make the campus a net contributor of electrical power to the regional grid. The first thought was the possibility of installing a fuel cell that would use solar energy during daylight hours to split water and make hydrogen, which would be used in the cell to make electricity when solar energy was not available. Although the technology now exists to do such things, at that time no commercial equipment was available at the scale we required, and that option had to be dropped.

But the possibility of storing energy by making hydrogen through the electrolysis of water persisted, and we explored pioneering in solar-electric hydrogen production with the idea that it could be used in internal combustion engines to displace fossil fuels. Although the evolution of that transition is inevitable, we were in 1998 well ahead of our time and that hope too fell by the wayside on the grounds of the practical difficulties and expense of the electrolysis of water and then storing the hydrogen under pressure. Marc Rosenbaum, our ultimate resource in engineering, estimated that we would require six large truck-sized tanks to store enough hydrogen at 150 pounds per square inch to be significant in our operation over just a few days without sun.

We moved on to accept that the best route at that time was photovoltaic panels and a wind turbine, if possible, connected through the existing power grid. Our rooftop invited solar-electric panels that could be arranged to send electricity back through our meter into the electric grid. The arrangement would reduce our meter reading and be the equivalent of selling our power back to the electric company at the same price we normally pay. A wind turbine could be added later. (See chapter IV for a more extensive discussion of energy.)

Meanwhile, we puzzled over designs for efficient heating. The tried and true design for comfortable living at forty-two degrees north on Cape Cod is the story-and-one-half Cape Cod cottage with a central chimney and a fireplace in every room (figure 3.2). The massive central chimney,

Figure 3.2 A Cape Cod cottage. The central chimney supported a fireplace in each room and the chimney's mass, once heated, lent stability to the heating system for the whole house. (Jonathan Kendrick House, State Highway, South Orleans. Historic American Buildings Survey, Arthur C. Haskell, Photographer, 1935. HABS, Mass 1-ORLS.1. Library of Congress)

once heated, kept the house warm in the winter despite the piercing winds and persistent cold of the New England coast. The fireplaces were fed with wood, locally available and, at least nominally, renewable in woodlots preserved for the purpose. Many New England towns established town woodlots, some of which persist today as public lands. It was a solar-powered heating system, simple, locally self-sufficient, reliable, and effective. The architecture was also simple and popular, and the plan was easily expanded as domestic needs grew. The design persists and remains attractive, compact, and efficient in use of materials and comfortable in all seasons. The design was used widely throughout New England and elsewhere even as coal and oil gradually replaced wood as the fuel of choice during the twentieth century.

As global demand for oil soars and supplies become conspicuously limited, the twenty-first century is bringing a new revolution away from oil and coal to enduring sources, especially solar energy in all its various forms. The innovations are profound in that they involve a shift away from combustion to heating with lower temperature heat sources and toward large reductions in demand for heat. This latter point requires advances in the conservation of energy: buildings must be much better insulated and far more leakproof than ever before so the demand for energy is much reduced. Marc Rosenbaum, our energy consultant, talks of construction that aims at a building capable of being heated by "one warm dog." The transitions in architecture include an interest in returning to the independence provided by the wood-fueled house of the past.

As we explored possibilities for heating without combustion, we added a heat pump with the possibility of using air as the vehicle for moving heat, as is commonly done with air conditioning, or groundwater as a source of heat to be transferred to air. We could, of course, use solar hot-water panels to heat water in a large tank in sufficient quantity to last over several days without bright sun. But the ground-source heat pump, tapping a large supply of groundwater from below the frost line, offered a greater potential as a source of heat than a limited array of solar hot-water panels. With both technologies low-temperature heat can be used very effectively in radiant energy systems throughout the living quarters. Instead of radiators scattered throughout a building, inexpensive plastic piping can be used to warm the entire floor area. (The use of plastic in this case avoids much more expensive copper pipes and simply shows the difficulties of meeting all the criteria so hopefully set forth originally.) These systems put a premium on tight, insulated windows with double or triple glazing. Such heating systems, combined with complementary innovations in energy-conserving construction, have brought a revolution in architecture that makes almost any configuration of construction possible and comfortable. Although the beauty and efficiency of the Cape Cod cottage remains a fundamental truth, modern architecture can wander far from that classic form and still improve on the New Englanders' essential conservatism.

DESIGNING WITH THE LAND

Ecologists delight in "reading the landscape" to infer its history and judge its potential at the moment. This area had been farmed for nearly 300 years following its settlement in the early 1600s. The transition from an agrarian landscape to a summer-residential landscape with small lots began early in the nineteenth century and accelerated through the twentieth. It was re-markable that we could still in 1998 purchase even a modest tract.

The purchase involved about eight acres in a roughly trapezoidal lot with several hundred feet of frontage on Woods Hole Road (figure 3.1). Hilltop House was served by a loop driveway that entered the tract on the curve in Woods Hole Road and followed an old road around the shoulder of the hill below the original house to the west. The old road originally served the farmstead just over the ridge beyond Hilltop House. The barn stands today, rebuilt by Charles Johnson as a substantial dwelling two de-cades before our interest in Quisset. The old road, cut into the steeply slop-ing land, was interrupted by the expansion of Hilltop House and deflected in front of the mansion into the loop drive. The segment of the old road where the slope was steep along the shoulder of the hill was protected above and below with retaining walls of cut granite, probably at the time the house was built in the 1870s. The granite was drilled and cut by hand, as was common at that time, from local stones glacially deposited. A dike in one stone in the woods near the bottom of the steep rise appears in one of the cut stones of the wall. The original driveway has been preserved but intersects the main road on a blind curve and is no longer used except for maintenance of the grounds.

Hilltop House occupied the very end of Quissett Ridge, the top of the moraine that drops steeply on the eastern end sixty feet to the bottom of a kettle hole. The contours of the ridge defined the potential for expansion of the building. Bill McDonough's analogy of a leaf reaching out into the sun was appropriate. The original house was to lose its unattractive rear wing to be replaced by an expansion of the building in the same outline.

We fitted the building to the contours of the land and designed the space we needed, expanding the four floors of Hilltop House. We could, of course, have moved the land around as is commonly done these days to accommodate a different building, lower and simpler and more easily constructed of local materials. We chose to respect the land, preserve its glacial contours and its historic road and commanding aspect. Our new wing was a comfortable fit with the rebuilt Victorian house and its surrounding porch. The wing was barely visible from the front and its plain, even severe, contemporary style fought not at all with the rebuilt Victorian mansion.

DESIGNING WITH "CODE"

Woods Hole is part of the Town of Falmouth and is of course required to follow the Falmouth zoning codes. Falmouth zoning laws set educational institutions beyond zoning restrictions. We had, years earlier, established with the town that the Woods Hole Research Center qualifies as an educational institution. Nevertheless, we decided that we should put all our activities under the scrutiny and provisions of the town's regulations, which are, after all, designed to protect each from all and all from each. We could not see why we should have a special exception. The town planning board quite properly referred our plans to the Cape Cod Commission, the Cape's land-use agency, which must by law review all plans for buildings in excess of 10,000 square feet as potential "Developments of Regional Impact." We were quickly granted exemption from this review by act of the Commission, whose members were delighted with our plans in all respects.

In the process of this review we agreed to set aside a fraction of the 8.1-acre tract as conservation land (figure 3.1) to be managed under the direction of our local land trust, the 300 Committee. That commitment became a formal conservation easement, protecting in perpetuity for conservation purposes 2.4 acres of forest at the far western end of our tract. We stipulated that the land would be managed under the advisement of the committee, although it is to be used for nature trails and for demonstrations of various techniques used in forest research. Most of these objectives are defined by the Town of Falmouth and stated explicitly in the town's "Comprehensive Park and Open Space Plan" (1986).

Through an interesting gift of adjacent land the eight acres we had purchased became nine acres and the Center gained access to a residential road near the northern boundary of the original tract. The land in question was a modest lot given by Dr. Laties and known as the Laties lot on Quissett Circle, a nearby residential development. The lot was below the minimum size for a house and could not be sold to advantage. Nevertheless, the owner was not interested in donating it to the center and the Center had little interest in purchasing it. By the Center's making a gift of a small piece of adjacent land, the lot was expanded to "buildable size," its value thereby increased to the point where its donation to the center was a tax advantage to the owner, who made the gift of the whole back to the Center. The Center gained access to Quissett Circle and the possibility of building there if necessary for whatever purpose might develop, such as housing students, new faculty, or guests.

In addition to zoning codes we also, of course, were at the mercy of building codes, which forced reconsideration of some of our goals. For example, in keeping with our objective to use local materials, we wanted to frame the new wing with white pine timbers cut and milled locally. Barns and other large buildings had been constructed locally for three centuries with such timbers. And a local industry was producing them now in Carver, Massachusetts, not far away. But practicality intruded immediately. The curving back facade was on a slope and difficult to construct in any case, and the size of the timbers intruded on the interior space. More than that, the wing was a full four floors and the strength of the construction with pine, even with large timbers, was lacking. The solution was an immediate reversion to a bolted and welded steel frame. The decision was a joint one among architects, builders, and owners. The only puzzle was why we had considered timber construction so carefully when it was in fact not practical, nor, I was told, was it consistent with building codes.

The building code hung as a cloud over everyone involved in the project at every step in design and construction. The official building code exists in writing, but the "code" also exists in the minds of town officers and architects and builders as a result of their practice and experience. No one on our staff was interested in delving into that morass, and we were, to all practical purposes, completely at the mercy of the experts whom we left to argue among themselves. The code emerged repeatedly, if not continuously, in our discussions and had profound effects at virtually every turn. It often seemed to emerge as a mysterious set of rules from mysterious committees that had proscribed in advance every possible innovation an owner might offer and most of the imaginative suggestions of architects. Discussions of what we might want as innovations often ended peremptorily with "code."

Although they can be inhibiting, the fact is that the codes have emerged from need. They are designed to protect the public from endangerment or fraud through sleaze and incompetence as well as bad design.

Much hinged on whether the building was to be public or private. The plan for public lectures made the whole auditorium "public" and triggered a new and more demanding set of regulations. Code, whatever the owners and the architect might have to say, then set the form of the building by defining the place and form of, for instance, stairways. Fire was the primary consideration, and stairways could act as chimneys and carry fire through two or three floors. The time of a grand staircase through the center of a public building had passed, and stairways now have to be isolated with fireproof doors and walls, whatever the everlasting inconvenience to dwellers. But we did arrange a central stairway that connected the ground or basement floor with the main floor and the third-floor bridge. The stairway, magnificent as it is, invites a guest to the upper floors. But arrival on the second floor, although offering grand interior and exterior views from the bridge, offers no clue as to the existence of another floor or how to find it. Initial reactions among those arriving for the first time on the bridge en route to the top floor range from puzzlement to frustration. Is it real? Where is it? How do I get there? The answer is in the code. Find a fireproof stairway down the hall in either direction.

No one was surprised that the code demanded a sprinkler system throughout the building, although the sprinkler emerged with no beauty at all, conspicuously anomalous black iron pipes in stairways and sprinkler heads in ceilings, threatening hydraulic disaster at the slightest misstep, an overheated room, smoke from a popcorn feast, or an unexpected mechanical misadventure. When we had digested all the details of the sprinkler system to black-iron perfection, we had a municipal specialist in code, the one who had approved the plans, come to voice his final, formal approval and allow the rest of the work on the building, delayed until the code had been satisfied, to proceed. The expert observed that our porches were not "sprinklered" and that they were extensive and flammable. Sprinklers are essential. Our water-filled system, already completed throughout the building, could not serve the porch because it would be outside and subject to freezing. The porch would require a special dry system, a completely new one, never anticipated by architects or envisioned by builders or owners or by the specialist in code who approved the plans. So a new, totally different system from the one we had was installed, tested, and set on its hair trigger. "Code, you know." And we ran more pipes and filled them with compressed air, which replaced the water. If a valve opened, the pressure would drop and water would come and do its duty on the porch. The whole water-restrained-on-a-hair-trigger system throughout the building, viewed in its stark reality, was a threat quite parallel to a thousand nuclear weapons on hair-trigger alert with no enemy in sight. But it was code, endorsed by the powers. And, as with nuclear weapons, all is for the common good. So we live with both.

Code had its personal side. Our builders meticulously, carefully, and efficiently scheduled the work. They had arranged subcontractors to appear at specific times to do specific things as construction proceeded logically from foundation to framing to roof to interior finishing. Electrical and plumbing contractors were to work after the building had been closed in while the extensive finish work on the outside was proceeding. But the electrical inspector had established his own personal rule that he would not inspect the electrical work and allow interior finishing to begin until the outside finish work had been completed, shingles were in place on the roof and siding, windows were complete, and trim was finished. No one involved in the scheduling of the work had been advised of this requirement and no one had encountered it previously. The requirement was unique to Falmouth and this inspector. The scheduling was in chaos. Subcontractors were themselves scheduled on other jobs and had to attempt to reschedule their work on very short notice. Weeks of delay ensued as we waited for the builders to come, accumulate materials long ordered for a different schedule, and complete the outside finish, not scheduled originally until much later. Expenses mounted. No entreaty to the inspector brought movement. We lived through the chaos, but chaos it was, all in defense of an inspector's interpretation of the code. In another circumstance in a larger world one could see how bribery emerges in the construction industry.

HISTORICAL INTERESTS

Historical issues are, and should be, considered in determining land uses. Most towns and states have historical commissions with varying official powers in planning and zoning. The Commonwealth of Massachusetts, with its deep roots in colonial history, is no exception, and the Town of Falmouth has similar pride and interests. The town has in fact established its own zoning plan with historical districts where special restrictions on construction apply. There is interest in the town that extends beyond these districts to touch almost any change in the older structures.

So it was with Hilltop House. The original summer house built for Helen Turner in 1877 on the eastern end of Quissett Ridge was on land purchased in 1875, probably from a larger tract owned by John Davis. The site was known from the beginning as "Hilltop" and, as the building was modified and its use expanded to accommodate guests, it became Hilltop House and later, the Rev-Kury cottage. Although the building's history was interesting, the structure was not of special architectural or historical interest. It was a spectacular landmark in a conspicuous place, a site visited by many over the years, and local interests in preserving the landmark were strong. We shared that interest and, afflicted with a New England conservatism and frugality, had no difficulty joining in the wish to save the building. The Massachusetts Historical Commission also took an explicit, if quite general, interest in its renovation. The Commission's approval was a requirement in dealing with the Commonwealth agencies we approached for financing. The approval was pro forma and required nothing from us but a letter expressing our intention, but a year passed before the Commission's note arrived and we were free to proceed with the blessing of all agencies. The decision to preserve the original structure brought some surprises and not a little reconsideration.

GAINING EXPERIENCE WITH OLD BUILDINGS

The newly purchased building, although in need of repair, was put to use immediately in support of the Center's program as an adjunct to the five sites[1] occupied in whole or in part in the village. Because there was no permanent or even daily occupancy we maintained the security alarm system established by the previous owners. We were concerned about vandalism of an apparently abandoned building and about the possibility of fire. Movement anywhere in the building triggered the alarm and brought a telephone call to the new owners, usually in the person of the director, who soon learned that raccoons had squatters' rights in this castle and would yield not at all to rational discussion as to actual ownership. We learned to live with them as regular occupants for a time.

Before we could begin to rehabilitate the existing structure, we had to address a few structural and equipment challenges. First was a failure of the hot-water system, an oil-fired water tank in the basement. A substantial water leak, which was in fact a broken pipe, filled the basement with water to a depth of twelve to fifteen inches and flooded the burner. The burner, however, continued to pump oil, which, floating on the water throughout the cellar, threatened a fire. As the water drained away into the sandy soil, the oil was carried with it and contaminated the entire cellar and the soil under the building. I discovered the catastrophe one Sunday evening a day or so after the break, when the cellar was draining about as fast as the water and oil flowed in. From the moment of discovery, codes and protocols took over. After a quick trip to my house in the village for rubber waders, I turned off the electrical power, the water, and the oil before the fire department arrived and the official machinery of such disasters began to operate.

The Falmouth Fire Department took an immediate interest and thought it might be good to get started on cleaning up the mess. Although it was late in the evening, an emergency crew from Clean Harbors was engaged and, in less than three hours, started the restoration by soaking up the oil on the surface of the water in absorbent pads. One might think that owners would have some control over costs and methods in such circumstances, but I quickly learned that protocol in such circumstances is in the hands of high priests of pollution and owners are there to sign and pay. There was no discussion. *Veni. Vidi. Vici.* The specialists arrived, several people dispersed with their special equipment, defined their own objectives and methods, set their own prices, and, after due course, picked up their gear and several barrels (all but one), and left a bill. Our chief financial officer, Robert Barry, entered immediately, to my great relief. He was experienced, calm, and wise, oil for troubled waters. He realized, and managed to persuade me, that the owner's only job was to pay, not to question or seek to learn anything, or challenge or argue, just to pay quietly, which we did, over several weeks until a special, new, expensive, third-party inspection determined that the site was in fact "clean" and had written it all down in a formal report.

This event was our introduction to environmental rules and codes which, we learned, are complex, sometimes esoteric, and the personal property of clans of specialists who come to interpret them and define the cure, the endpoint of the cure, and the price. Although we support these rules in general, we were surprised by the extent of the bureaucracy and linked commerce now established around them. The final report was entitled "Class A-2 Response Action Outcome Statement Report" and was a full half-inch thick with more than one hundred pages of text that matched the title for clarity and interest and treated all aspects of the disaster. When I wondered aloud who, if anyone, reads such documents, Mr. Barry said that this report could, if I could suppress any scholarly curiosity and behave, be the end—the period at the end of the sentence that had started weeks before, had cost us at least $10,000, and resulted in the most thorough cleanup possible. Further questions were out of order. And the barrel of "contaminated waste" left by Clean Harbors was ours to find a way to dispose of, at extra cost.

But the experience with codes and rules was only the beginning. Most of the expense of this unfortunate oily experience was covered by insurance thoughtfully arranged by Mr. Barry, well in advance. The experience with codes, code officers, and interpretation of rules and laws, and the cures and those who define and work them, although our first in this project, proved highly useful.

From oil contamination we moved quickly to asbestos. The ancient furnace, a steam boiler recessed in a special narrow cavity in the floor of the ample cellar, was unquestionably a hazard, although still operating and protecting the building from freezing in winter. Just how it operated was not clear, but it did seem to be effective. It was conspicuously old, obviously neglected, and encrusted with decades of sedimented dust and dirt. Fearful of what one might discover with even casual scouting, no one was inclined to make its acquaintance. I did get close enough to the furnace pit finally to discover that under the crusts of dust and dirt the furnace and all the pipes associated with it were coated with soft asbestos insulation. Asbestos dust is an unquestionably hazardous material and can be produced in abundance from the type of soft, unpainted insulation packed around every pipe in the basement that had anything to do with our large steam heating system.

It was essential that the asbestos hazard be removed. Handling asbestos in such circumstances is also a highly demanding specialized challenge. Again, there is a protocol and a priesthood. Again, I called on our distinguished and resourceful financial officer, Robert Barry, to engage the priests who, in space suits and breathing through elaborate filters, carefully removed the asbestos without generating a toxic cloud, filtered the basement air and carried the asbestos off to a permanent, secure, and safe dump. There were, of course, large fees, but the entire process led to the disappearance of the boiler and its web of asbestos- and dust-covered pipes, all done with quiet efficiency and with carefully planned containment of every hazard and potential hazard. The priesthood was well trained and effective and, as strange as it may seem to have to find expensive specialists to clean up the cellar, they were essential and operated with skills bordering on grace. All of this activity was prelude to permission to begin construction.

DECONSTRUCTION AND RECONSTRUCTION

The initial plan was a simple, clever, highly efficient, economically attractive addition to the existing building. The plan was developed early in considerable detail and met our stated objectives of compact efficiency. It was so cleverly efficient and so precisely fit the requirements that it exuded sterility through every pore. We had not asked to be inspired, but we expected to be, despite our lack of imagination and flair. But we were saved from the embarrassment of confessing that we needed more color in our design.

The hilltop drops away immediately behind the existing main building, and the back of the new building as drawn would require reconfiguring the hill and constructing a very high cement supporting wall as the back of the addition, a cliff of thirty feet or more. Although the regular, rectangular building met our requirements and appealed to some as convenient and economically attractive, the construction of a concrete cliff as the back foundation appealed to no one. Biophysical reality again forced it-

Figure 3.3 Deconstruction of Hilltop House. The structure required a little more renovation than anyone had anticipated.

self into the planning. An alternative and more appropriate plan emerged quickly, a plan that followed the contours of the ridge with a graciously curving wing that flowed almost naturally from the existing structure. The Victorian house had three floors above the basement, and the new wing would follow the same pattern with the expanded basement floor at ground level looking out into the several acres of woodland behind the building.

As the reconstruction of the 1877 mansion proceeded, the confidence of the experts who had examined its structural integrity began to wilt (figures 3.3 and 3.4). The initial deconstruction revealed the need for more deconstruction, and major reconstruction became an urgent necessity, far beyond our plan. The experts had done the best they could, but at best they offered guesses and they were mistaken. But that conclusion was ex

$100 FINE
FOR UTTERING THE
FOLLOWING PHRASE:

"...THE BUILDING
SHOULD HAVE BEEN
TORN DOWN...."

Figure 3.4 Sign in the construction office.

post facto. The problems were several and emerged serially. They ranged from inconveniences to fundamentals. It was in fact a summer house, inexpensively framed using "balloon" construction with floors hung from light timbers running sill to eves, two, and in some places, three, floors. No one had guessed that there would be a need for extensive replacement of rotten or unspliced "floating" sills. Replacing those sills required in the end the reconstruction of major segments of the building.

But the most threatening development that nearly destroyed the residue of the structure that had survived to that point was the discovery of loose-flowing sand underlying the foundation at the back of the building where the back wing was removed. The threat was that the sand might simply flow out from under the residual shell and leave us with nothing but a pile of used lumber. There were many hours when the survival of the stripped-down shell of the mansion was in question and the safety of the workers was a serious issue. This problem was crowned with the discovery of a very large boulder where the base of the elevator was to be placed. The combination presented a major challenge, first in shoring up the building as the kitchen wing was removed and the entire back of the building opened to make way for the foundation of the new wing, and then in removing the giant boulder without causing further destruction.

The lessons were few except that all construction projects encounter problems that emerge as surprises no matter how comprehensive the planning. In this project our wish to conserve as much of the original structure as possible proved far more difficult, time-consuming, expensive, and even dangerous, than anticipated. The unanticipated expenses were in the installation of a steel supporting structure under emergency conditions and the removal of the most inconveniently placed giant glacial boulder. The expenses fell to the contractor under our contract.

My own limited experience led me to anticipate that the boulder would be removed after having been split with a modest charge of dynamite. I was mistaken. The technology for such matters had advanced far beyond my ken. The boulder was drilled expertly and split using a compressed air system that was rapid, quiet, effective, and safe. It produced fractured granite that was later used in attractive stonework on the site. No blasting was required at any point. The building did not collapse, or even move significantly. Construction marched on.

THE EFFECTS OF AUTOMOBILES ON ARCHITECTS

The decision to move from the village of Woods Hole to a campus in Quissett was a move to the suburbs. In making such a move we made a commitment to commuting, usually by car, at least for the moment, although one of the points we made in justifying this site was its proximity to the bicycle path that follows the one-time railroad track between Woods Hole and Falmouth. As to automobile access, municipal codes set standards involving roads and parking. Parking is a major land use, whatever we might wish. A person with a car occupies more space in the parking lot than in the building. And the area assigned to each car is defined by the town parking regulations, substantially by law, based on the space in the building. Despite our eight acres we found the area required for parking under town rules demanding, even excessive. Inside the building people can be treated quite callously according to code, at least by comparison with their cars, which get a defined minimum space outside.

A parking lot is not commonly the most admirable element of the landscaping and we sought to limit the intrusion there, especially in a circumstance where the large setback from the road offered an attractive perspective across a field. The hill does offer a shelf ten to fifteen feet below and behind the top of the rise beyond the building site. Used for parking, it would be invisible from the front and convenient to the building. It was, however, small by comparison with the need and awkward of access. We soon ruled it out while struggling with the best arrangement in front of the building that would meet our needs attractively and the demands of the Town of Falmouth as well. The solution was a curving drive with angled parking along one side and supplemental parallel parking along the other. In addition, under pressure we agreed with the town to grade the lower part of the front of the lot behind the stone retaining wall along the main road so cars might be parked there on occasion. The whole became a major project, a topic of negotiation with the town and a topic of considerable interest within the staff.

There were many voices that competed with the voice of the landscape architect. What emerged was a gracefully curved driveway that was to be paved with asphalt for stability, but the parking areas on both sides of the drive were to be gravel held in place by a newly developed porous matting that was installed and covered with pea-sized gravel. The system appears functional and stable after four years' use. On this one we had our way, helped by a knowledgeable builder.

The plan was to have the paved portion of the drive drain across the drive into the porous angled parking area. Any excess runoff in large storms was to flow across the parking area into a grassed drainage leading to a sump close to the main road below. The sump protected the main road and the neighbors from any excess runoff not contained by the combination of a porous parking area, a grassed drainage, and the woodland beyond. Our engineer, who had the force of the town officials behind him, insisted over my objections that the sump be built. It remains today, a stoned-up dry pond. The stone is broken granite, beautifully variegated, from the granite found on the site in the form of giant boulders that had to be broken, as was the boulder at the base of the elevator shaft. The pond had water in it for a short time once over a four-year period when four to six inches of rain were recorded in various parts of the town within twenty-four hours. Otherwise, the porous parking area and the grassed seepage area and woods beyond provide adequate area for infiltration.

Lighting of the new parking area, so prominently a part of the view of the building from almost any direction, was a special challenge. The objective was beauty, functionality, and efficiency. After much research and discussion with architects, gracefully curved lighting fixtures were found that provided subdued lighting from shielded compact fluorescent bulbs. The lighting was judged adequate and brought enthusiastic approval from historical and other local interests that saw the fixtures as a model for the emerging era of lower energy use. The combination of low light intensity, gracefully shielded fixtures, and the curving driveway leading to a building surrounded by an inviting porch presents an unusually attractive evening view for those passing on the road below. Finished, it brought flattery from local friends. (Such flattery does not hinder fund-raising, and we felt that our struggles in design were warranted and may well have been rewarded.)

THE PATHS AND THE ROCK GARDEN

Plans for the landscaping incorporated the paths and a picnic area on the knoll immediately in front of the building. The area is "the rock garden," connected by a graveled path to the building. The rocks are large glacial boulders from the site, and the path loops through and around them.

The material for the various paths attracted considerable interest in that there was antipathy among all to concrete or tar surfaces in any place where they could be avoided. Concrete was, obviously, necessary for the long entrance ramp, but other walks were to be gravel. Fine gravel, however, was ruled unacceptable as difficult to walk on and liable to be tracked easily into the building. Unfortunately, the builders purchased and had delivered a large load of expensive, very fine gravel to be used in all the walks. The gravel was unsuitable, but the load persisted through extensive objections and much discussion that was the more difficult because there was no clearly defined alternative that was attractive despite the early identification of the issue.

The resolution emerged when the subcontractor who was pouring cement and laying the asphalt driveway suggested washed concrete, which reveals the coarse glacial gravel used in cement but keeps it bound. The surface is colorful, attractive, and inexpensive. It appealed immediately to all. The fine gravel was banned and used for the walks in the rock garden, well away from the building. The nearby walks were washed concrete and the long path around the building was coarse gravel, quite suitable for walking and too coarse to track into the building. The deep, fine gravel of the rock garden paths remains a mistake—one of few. The gravel is present in excess, a coarse quicksand, very fine and difficult to walk in. Walking there provides an unusual, energetic experience, equivalent to struggling uphill when in fact walking downhill, and clearly illustrates why it was banned on all other paths. It is one of the memorable features of the Ordway Campus rock garden—a mistake, too small to correct, but too conspicuous to ignore. It appeared toward the end of construction when we were tallying the costs, assembling lists of final details called "punch lists," and exploring the limit of accommodation with architects and builders and trying to schedule the very end. Although the rock garden was a landmark, the gravel in the paths was a small issue. Much bigger was the bottom line of construction, the question how much we had spent on all this green architecture and whether it was worth it in the short-term context or the long. Was it wise, or simply expensive, to try to save the old building? Was the entire venture worth the effort?

POLLUTION: A CHEMICAL HOOD VIOLATES PRINCIPLES OF ZERO RELEASE

I recall a special series of lectures that I joined in offering at Argonne National Laboratory many years ago with Alvin Weinberg, among others. Weinberg was then the director of Oak Ridge National Laboratory and one of my heroes. The lectures were for selected undergraduate students from around the nation.

I presented a vigorous argument that the only way that we could make a world that would continue to function as a human habitat was to adopt a policy of "zero release" of toxic substances for all of industry and other human activities. Weinberg, ever practical and compromising, was appalled that I was making such, to him, outlandish statements to impressionable young students, even though he was an outspoken and effective critic of policies that would expose the public to ionizing radiation from bombs or reactors. I argued that in effect we had, and have now, a zero-release policy for radionuclides from reactors, but Weinberg, for all his brilliance, had not thought of it that way. Years later as we continued the discussion, he ultimately agreed that the ecologist and biologist (namely me) had a serious point, impractical though it seemed.

I continue to believe that with respect to chemical and many other "wastes" we should subscribe to a zero-release standard,[2] violating it only under carefully defined conditions when we can demonstrate that in fact no biotic hazard exists. I use two examples. First, DDT and its breakdown products are accumulated so rapidly and effectively into living systems, and last so long, that there is no possibility of defining a "safe" level of use in the open environment. Concentration factors of hundreds of thousands–fold are common, and people are inescapably a part of the food web. There is no use that avoids this hazard, including the unwise but widely touted use in attempting to protect people from malaria in the tropics. There are other means for avoiding mosquitoes in the tropics. Second, with radioactive isotopes such as strontium and cesium, which behave as calcium and potassium in living systems, we accept the challenge of containing them and other radionuclides as part of the technology and basic rules of operation of reactors.

A zero-release rule is the only practical reality, not the dream of an idealist scientist. There is no hope of chasing every potential chemical release from industrial activities globally, defining its hazards, and making a judgment as to its safety.[3] The rule must be no release. The chemistry of the earth is a sacred trust, to be preserved intact and inviolate, if we are to continue to have a biotically mediated and safe world. We confront almost daily new mysteries as to why populations of apparently healthy species are crashing. At the moment of this writing the news is reporting the unexplained mortality of bats over large areas in the eastern United States. There is a specific cause, I suppose, but it is no surprise that this is happening. There is such a myriad of changes in the chemistry of environment, not to speak of the biophysics of climate, that virtually every species is living on the edge of one environmental disaster or another, just as the full range of species of the salt marshes of Long Island accumulated residues of DDT through many factors of ten to lethal levels. All surviving individuals we collected at every step in the food web carried concentrations within one factor of ten of acute lethality.[4] That extraneous hazard was in addition to all the other normal hazards of life and other pollutants.

The zero-release civilization becomes the only way, on close examination, to create a world that works, and the principle is obviously to be extended to architecture and to chemical laboratories in general.

We sought to live by such a standard here. But the challenge was large and the solutions too immature at the moment. The jump was just too big for us. We were forced to accept that laboratories that use at any time, or even just might use, toxins that might contaminate the air of the laboratory,

Figure 3.5 The exhaust for the hood in the chemical laboratory had to be installed after the rooftop electrical panels. The tank in the background to the right is a large town-owned water tank on a rise to the northward behind the building.

even temporarily, require a system for diluting and exhausting the noxious materials for the safety of the people in the lab. The standard safety device for preventing air contamination is a chemical hood, designed to allow the restriction of the potential contamination to a small, confined volume in the laboratory and to exhaust it immediately outside the building in a place where it will be diluted to innocuousness, at least as far as people are concerned (figure 3.5). In the larger context the chemical enters the circulation of the atmosphere, where it may be degraded photochemically, washed out in rain, condensed into the Arctic cold, or carried by air or water or sediments into the oceans. A chemical hood was standard, and we had to have one. It was in a class with the plastic piping and the neutralizing tanks that were ultimately required by the plumbing inspector as discussed below.

Our experience with the hood was almost humorous. Once we accepted the need for a more or less standard chemical hood in the laboratory on the top floor of the new building, we assumed that finding a passage for the vent through the roof above would be a simple matter. Although the hood was defined in the plans, the route for its exhaust around the rooftop solar panels could not immediately be defined and was not drawn. In fact, by the time the laboratory and the entire wing had been completed, the exhaust had not been designed and the hood, although present, was not functional. Forgetting the exhaust for the hood was not only simple, it was clearly desirable in the eyes of all but the owners, who despite their general antipathy toward such releases had come to the unavoidable decision that a chemical hood, if it existed at all, should be vented outside the building.

The solution was ex post facto to engage a specialist to find a way through the elaborate bracing of the roof, around the array of solar panels, to a spot on the northern edge of the roof for the blower and exhaust, a miniature rocket in appearance, firing unknown chemicals into an unsuspecting and helpless biosphere. It had to be north of the panels to avoid casting a shadow on them and had to be carried there in small pieces along the residual margin of the roof not covered with solar collectors. Beyond the challenge of place for the exhaust, the hood had to function correctly and not present a serious problem in winter by exhausting a disproportionate fraction of the heated air of the institution. Its existence is a testimony to the difficulties inherent in realizing a strict zero-release policy, even in a simple chemical laboratory designed by experts aware of the challenge and willing to face it directly.

DESIGNING FOR ALL USERS

What codes did not define, safety or common sense often did. The building was open to the public, although privately owned. The public includes small children and the infirm. There were scores of issues where special circumstances had to be considered. A very attractive second-floor bridge required a fence for safety along both sides. The architects designed stainless steel cables tightly strung between uprights. The design was attractive, but the possibility of a child's climbing on the cables, or slipping between them, quickly demanded something less of a hazard. Tempered glass plates were much more expensive but also attractive, and safe. The first time I saw a toddler make a quick, independent scramble to the stairway, I appreciated those expensive, impregnable, confining glass plates lining the stairway and the bridge.

BACK TO THE ENERGY CHALLENGE

Energy and the conservation of energy entered virtually every issue and captured and controlled many topics at every stage of the construction. Windows had to be tight and double glazed where they were not triple glazed, as they were on the north side. Special thought had to be given to allow no uninsulated pockets in walls and no passages for leakage of outside air into wall spaces around doors or windows. Air and air flow was to be managed and carefully controlled as part of the energy budget of the building. And it was the energy budget that became the dominating influence on the entire process and the core issue in defining what would work and what would not. Clearly, salvaging a relict building and converting it to contemporary standards, accommodating codes, and meeting our own new expectations for energy and structural integrity, all emerged as expensive indulgences of historical interests that in the end slipped into a very attractive contemporary approximation of the Victorian mansion we started with.

Now it is time to look further into energy.

4

ENERGY IN A NEW WORLD

The energy squeeze of the early 1970s brought almost immediately the production of smaller, more fuel-efficient cars, a fifty-five mile per hour speed limit in the United States, and, in the Carter administration, subsidies for residential use of solar hot water and heating and for improvements in home insulation. It also brought a host of innovations in pricing of energy to reduce peak loads on power plants and reduce the need for expensive extra capacity to cover very short periods of high demand. The responses were appropriate and effective. The issue was covered in detail in the 1980 report of the President's Council on Environmental Quality, the *Global 2000 Report,* which defined the transitions in energy production and use that had to occur in the last two decades of the second millennium. The Reagan administration, inaugurated in 1981, scorned that report and all of the progress made toward developing solar energy, including the new and highly promising nationally financed Solar Energy Research Institute in Golden, Colorado.

Now, close to the end of the first decade of the third millennium, the climate-energy crunch is far more serious, clearly an immediate and long-term challenge, and our governmental leadership during the intervening years far, far behind what we had in 1980 at the end of the Carter administration. It has been a shameful and hugely expensive retrenchment, arrogant and deliberate, carried out despite abundant warnings from the scientific and scholarly community and summarized in scores of excellent tracts widely published and even discussed at length in the U.S. Congress and beyond.[1] A new, young, and talented president now seems certain to move the nation and the world forward again, but he cannot recover the losses of those nearly three decades.

Worse, although more than 180 nations signed and later ratified the 1992 Framework Convention on Climate Change, they chose to do nothing in fact to check the gathering storm. The ratifiers included the United States. The virtually universal ratification made it both national and international law that all nations individually and collectively act to "stabilize" the heat-trapping gases in the atmosphere at levels that would protect "human interests" and "nature." The United States, although it should have taken international leadership, later scorned that treaty and scorned the implementing agreement under the treaty, the Kyoto Protocol of 1997, which was negotiated specifically to meet the demands of the United States. To the extent that progress has been made in this first decade of the new millennium toward implementing the protocol in the United States, the progress has been through bottom-up efforts, piecemeal national laws and most recently regional plans for reducing use of fossil fuels by states such as California and the northeastern states, as well as scores of local efforts, all emerging from frustration with the lack of national leadership. As the prices of fossil fuels have risen, alternatives have become more economically attractive and commercial initiatives are expanding to conserve fossil fuels and, even more importantly, to exploit wind and other sources of solar energy directly. The new president seems poised to add new momentum to this transition, which is inevitable and welcome.

One of the most fascinating aspects of the latter half of the twentieth century was the extent to which the ordinary citizen did not need to think about energy at all. We were in the midst of the fossil-fueled age and inexpensive energy was freely available. Coal and oil and gas were easily transported and easily burned. They displaced wood for heat, even when wood was available nearby at little or no monetary cost. Automobile travel was inexpensive. Gasoline was cheaper than bottled water. We could afford to spread our living quarters out over the landscape and commute miles by car to work in the city. Electricity, too, was inexpensive, mostly generated, then and still, by burning coal or oil or gas, in giant central power plants. The power is distributed into an all-encompassing electrical grid that actually receives power from many such plants and distributes it according to needs. The fossil-fuel energy was cheap enough that there was little or no competition from any other source, even from a potentially infinite source such as wind or sun. More than that, the energy came in compact forms that could be easily stored or carried around as coal or oil or liquefied gas. Wind and sun are only intermittently available and by comparison, diffuse, inconvenient, and expensive to harness. The ubiquity and convenience of the fossil fuel–based industrial society was such that we could ignore the details of its function and assume that our comfortable world would continue indefinitely and could be improved routinely and expanded indefinitely by further applications of energy through ever more ingenious technology.

The process for exploiting fossil energy grew and became large—very large. Even by global standards, it was large. Before we really knew what we were doing, and certainly without a deliberate plan, we were performing a change in the earth's systems of geological proportions, moving into the atmosphere in one year billions of tons of carbon stored in the earth's crust over hundreds of millions of years and releasing it largely as carbon dioxide. In a bit more than one century we increased the carbon dioxide in the atmosphere by forty percent and triggered an open-ended warming of the earth, a profound and continuing disruption of climate globally. Our experiment, thoughtless as it was, turned out to be a rash venture, a one-way ticket off the earth, if we were to allow it to continue. By the latter half of the twentieth century the changes in climate had become clear enough that the scientific community had confirmed the need to bring an early end to the fossil-fuel age despite the momentum of the economic and political systems, all supported by cheap fossil energy.

The end of the fossil-fuel age appears now, in the early years of the third millennium, to be well underway, with the revolution bubbling up from the bottom as the era of oil had its own beginnings with oil seeps in

Pennsylvania. The design and construction of the Ordway Campus was a small local step in the transition. We drew on a wealth of experience, much dating from the Carter years and before when there was a surge of interest, led by the president himself. The tax subsidies in those years stimulated research, experimentation, and publications that brought innovations in solar energy installations, especially domestic hot-water systems, passive solar heating, superinsulation for conservation of energy in new buildings, and improvements in details of construction to make buildings far more efficient. Not surprisingly, many of the staff accumulated by the Center for research in environmental science had participated in those innovations. The staff brought a wealth of thoughtful experience and vigorous interest to the design of the new campus. I had myself with our son, John, then in college, designed and built in 1984 a twenty-five–panel hot-water heating system for our house at forty-two degrees north in Woods Hole. It has been operating highly successfully for more than two decades, producing domestic hot water throughout the year and heating critical segments of the house, except for ten to sixteen weeks during the depths of the New England winter, when days are short and northwest winds bring the cold of the persistent Canadian high.

By the time we were ready to proceed with our experiment in modern construction, we—our staff and trustees and immediate friends and colleagues—had accumulated additional experience, assembled background information on the site, and explored every channel we could imagine to make this building independent of outside sources of energy, including fossil fuels and electricity normally used in such buildings. We knew that heating and cooling and ventilation and the demand for hot water in office buildings commonly sums to fifty percent or more of their total use of energy (figure 4.1). It was clear that there were also substantial improvements to be made in the efficiency of energy use in lighting (as we did with the outdoor lighting of the driveway) and in the equipment used in the buildings, including computers.

We had dreamed of, and explored, the possibilities of jumping immediately to independence from the oil-ensnared world through development

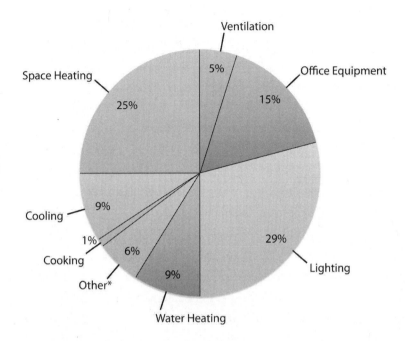

Figure 4.1   Breakdown of energy use in office buildings. *Source:* Energy Information Administration, 1995 Commercial Buildings Energy Consumption Survey.

of a hydrogen-based economy, at least in our small segment of the world, by generating an excess of electrical energy and using the excess to split water and store energy as hydrogen for use in a fuel cell. "Independence" to us meant "off the grid"—completely independent—if we managed things correctly. But off the grid certainly involved a need to store energy. We had long been aware of the possibilities of using hydrogen as a storage medium. Electrical energy produced in excess of immediate needs can be used to split water, and the hydrogen can be captured and stored under pressure for later use, either in combustion or in a fuel cell. Although internal combustion engines can be adjusted with comparative ease to run on hydrogen, the fuel cell technology was not yet easily available at a scale appropriate for our use. More than that, the storage of a sufficient volume of hydrogen to meet anticipated needs even for internal combustion engines was seen as awkward and expensive in money and energy under the very best circumstances, at least at the moment. We, acting alone, could not make the jump to hydrogen. That jump would require governmental leadership and planning. The alternative for off the grid was batteries, which are expensive to install, require maintenance, and ultimately require renewal. Again, we were not prepared for that technology and responsibility in maintenance. Much more attractive was the idea of remaining on the grid while generating an excess of energy that might be returned to the power company for a fee, or used on-site.

A combination of solar panels and a wind turbine seemed ideal in that, at forty-two degrees north on the New England coast, the winter winds pick up as the solar input drops. Our analyses became more realistic and practical as we accumulated experience in an able staff that eagerly soaked up information from every source. Members of our staff became top-level experts, studying at the knee of energy consultant Marc Rosenbaum and experts from the McDonough architectural group. We sought interest and advice from the Massachusetts Renewable Energy Trust (MRET), which had been established to manage a multimillion-dollar fund collected as a small surcharge on electrical bills in Massachusetts, a charge previously approved by the voters. The Trust was at that time just starting its operation, and we went to them ultimately with two proposals. The proposals were the products of research on energy use in buildings and on energy systems. Although the topic was new to us, experience had accumulated over years in the literature and we were able to call on special software, Energy-10, published by the Passive Solar Industries Council (ASHRAE)[2] to produce two models (table 4.1), one of a "standard" building of the dimensions we proposed—the base case—and the other of our Ordway Campus building, including the innovations envisioned. The model projected a demand for the Ordway Campus, if we followed our plan, of less than twenty percent of the demand of standard construction. A different model from the Energy Information Administration[3] based on contemporary designs yielded simi-

TABLE 4.1   A comparison of energy requirements of buildings constructed using standard techniques (base case) with the plans for the Ordway Building. The estimates were based on models widely used for this purpose. The plans reduced the requirements for energy to about one-fifth of those associated with standard construction techniques according to these appraisals. The appraisals proved surprisingly accurate.

		kWh/yr	BTU/ft^2/yr	kWh/ft^2/yr
Base Case	(1) ASHRAE	473,000	84,000	24.6
	(2) EIA 1995	501,000	89,000	26.1
Ordway Plan	(1) ASHRAE	90,000	16,000	4.66

lar base case estimates that a standard building would consume more than five times the energy we estimated for our new building.

The first proposal to the MRET was an attractive, integrated "whole building" design to address the range of issues inherent in our "zero net energy" goal in particular. The second was a proposal for a wind turbine discussed below. Although we were well aware at that time of efforts led largely by staff of the Natural Resources Defense Council and the U.S. Green Building Council to develop objective standards for construction of such buildings, those efforts were still in development and the complexities of our project, involving use of an existing building as well as new construction, persuaded us that we could not at that early stage join in the program that became LEED,[4] despite our enthusiasm for it.

Our goals in dealing with energy were set forth in the first proposal to the MRET:

The building was designed with the specific intent of producing, on a net annual basis, more energy than it consumes, and to accomplish this goal without burning any fossil fuel on site. With this aim in mind, we had to focus first on achieving efficiency in energy usage in the key areas of lighting, plug loads, and temperature control, which account for as much as seventy-nine percent of the average office energy load.

We analyzed a number of strategies for achieving desirable energy conservation and efficiency, and elected to

- optimize the use of natural lighting throughout the facility for both energy efficiency and aesthetics;
- use highly efficient insulation and window glazings designed to have low thermal emissivity and high light transmission;
- employ enthalpy wheels for the recovery of heat from the ventilation system. These wheels are porous ceramic that absorbs heat and water vapor from exhaust air at one point in its rotation and restores that energy to input air in another segment of rotation;
- minimize electrical, heating, and cooling loads by eliminating redundant electrical equipment (e.g., printers, copiers, and fax machines), by encouraging energy-conscious user behavior, and by using energy-efficient building systems, fixtures, and equipment;
- use thermal blinds and shutters in key locations to control unwanted solar gain;
- use thermal energy, collected from the ground using ground-source heat pumps, to cool and heat the building;
- employ a solar hot water system for our domestic hot water supply
- install a 26.4kWp (kilowatts peak) photovoltaic array.

The question that was raised repeatedly, and is still brought forth regularly, is the cost. An oil-based heating system is less expensive to install than any combination of active renewable energy systems with similar capacity. How can one justify a more expensive installation that appears to be more complicated, involves collecting diffuse supplies of energy, requires more careful and expensive construction, and relies on esoteric technologies that may not be obviously effective in the short term?

The answer has many parts, of course. One is that we build for the long term, decades to a century, perhaps, and we can anticipate changes in prices, in availability of resources, and in attitudes and laws. The climatic disruption that threatens us all will persist into the indefinite future and is abundant evidence that we have already outrun the capacity of the global environment to accommodate the continued use of fossil fuels. Major climatic changes have captured us all in a web of disruption that will only tighten around us and become more costly in money and lives with time. At the moment it takes monumental foolishness to ignore the transition and commit institutions to outmoded systems in new buildings that will be increasing financial and environmental liabilities decade by decade until, at great expense, they are rebuilt or replaced. But even more obvious is the conspicuous foolishness in allowing an unbridled exponential expansion of use of finite supplies of oil and gas and coal, all poisoning an also obviously finite human habitat threatened as well by other soaring chronic insults. A new course is imperative and the scientific community must lead. So ran our logic as we proceeded with what was in fact a great experiment, the largest and riskiest that we had so far undertaken. As the price of oil has soared over recent years we appreciated the thought and imagination that made our jump to self-sustaining sources of energy possible.

Our goal of "no combustion on-site" presented a major challenge for heating and electrical power. We were led early to the ground-source (using groundwater) heat pump system discussed below. The system is electrically powered and designed to feed warm water to radiant convectors (small, finned, copper pipe radiators) mounted high along the wall just below the ceiling in each room.

Such convectors operate on small differences in temperature and can be effective only in buildings that have a low demand for energy. They are in fact convective heaters that warm a layer of more or less stationary air high in the room. The convectors and the warm air high in the room radiate heat to the living space below and warm people directly just as the radiant heat we feel from the sun or from an open fireplace. The concept runs counter to the experience of most who have been accustomed to convective heaters mounted close to the floor and designed to warm the air low in the room, allowing it to rise by convection because it is lighter than cooler air and thereby circulating through the room. It took substantial effort on the part of Marc Rosenbaum to persuade us all, in particular me, that "valance convectors" would in fact warm the room with radiant heat. The key was a very tight building that actually required very little heat. Experience has proven him correct, despite rampant and persistent skepticism. The heaters provide radiant heat from above that is far more subtle than the abundant warmed air we are accustomed to from baseboard radiators. In this tight and well insulated building all exchanges with the outside are controlled. Again, the energy issues could not be separated from the details of construction. The critical fact is that a ground-source heat pump works with small differences in temperature and the system can be used only in circumstances where the requirements for heat are modest in a very well insulated and aerodynamically tight building.

Obtaining a tight outer shell for the building against the winter gales of the New England coast was a significant challenge for the builders, who had little experience with our demands. They joined in the project, however, with vigor and imagination, anticipating that they were on the edge of a revolution in construction. They appreciated the scrutiny and interest of a technically well qualified scientific staff as well as architects and advisors. It was the builders who led us to the highly effective foam insulation with the trade name Icynene®, an isocyanate liquid spray. The liquid, a two-part foam, mixed at application, immediately expands one hundredfold or more. It cannot be sprayed into closed areas for the expansion is enough to crack plaster or lift boards. But it can be sprayed to fill between studs, the excess cut away, and any hole filled on a second pass before the interior sheathing is installed. Walls filled with Icynene® are dead to sound and draft-free. Two men in coveralls worked their way around the building filling all outer walls and joints where small perforations often occur and allow drafts to enter the frame of the building. The result was an astonishingly tight and quiet building with interior walls constructed with offset studding to further isolate sounds as well as heat. The discovery of Icynene® and its generous use throughout sealed the building, provided thermal insulation, a vapor and gas barrier, and soundproofing.

Recent innovations in the construction of windows made a parallel improvement in the control of air in the building. The first principle was that the windows be tight when closed. Second, enough windows must open to ventilate the building on demand. Third, they must limit losses of radiant heat. For the large windows on the north side, triple-glazed argon-filled panels were used. All other windows were double-glazed. Each type has been designed to include a thermal break (space) between the outer metal cladding and the inner wooden frame. Our experience over four years with these windows has been exemplary. The critical test is the large, north-facing window that extends two floors in the main room at the bridge between the old and new buildings. On the coldest winter days there is no sensible cold-air drainage from that window. To one brought up in New England houses, such efficiency in heat management is spectacular. The windows meet the requirements of impermeability and insulation under the most trying conditions of our climate. Enough windows open to ventilate the building on the warmest days.

THE HEATING SYSTEM

There was never much question as to how to heat the building. The local landscape is rich with imaginative and surprisingly effective solar heating ventures. One of the simplest was installed by a well-known physical oceanographer, William Von Arx who, during the late 1970s and early 1980s following the energy crunch, took advantage of his south-sloping land to heat water from a shallow well in summer by circulating it through a black plastic pipe laid out on the ground. The warmed water was returned to the well. He built up thereby a superheated body of glacial till, which he tapped directly for heat during the winter. The system was so effective that the gas company mounted, to the lasting delight of Dutchman Von Arx, a special investigation to determine how Von Arx was managing to "cheat" them of gas sales.

Our approach was more complicated but also relied on the groundwater as a source of energy.[5] A 1,200-foot well provided a large source of groundwater that normally comes from the well at about fifty-four degrees Fahrenheit. The pump in the well, below the surface of the standing water column, circulates water continuously through the coils of the compressor (figure 4.2). That water can be cooled using ordinary refrigeration equipment and the heat transferred to heat the building. The water, taken from the depths of the well and cooled by a few degrees, is returned to the top of the well to start on the cycle again, warmed on its way to the bottom. The refrigeration equipment is similar to what is used in domestic refrigerators. The principle of operation involves the absorption and release of energy through the shift from a liquid phase to vapor and back to liquid.

It is, for example, the vaporization of water that absorbs much of the radiant solar energy of the tropics and keeps the interior of a moist forest cool. The vapor, warmed, rises and moves from the forest to higher altitudes and from the tropics toward the poles, where it is cooled and condenses. The heat of vaporization is released and the new locale, in this case the higher latitudes, is warmed. The process explains why the temperature changes in the tropics are small and the changes in the middle and higher latitudes are large as the earth warms.

In refrigeration compressors, nonaqueous chemicals, usually chlorofluorocarbon compounds that are liquid at room temperatures, are used because they have appropriate physical characteristics. The vaporization of the liquid as it is warmed absorbs heat from the well water and cools it. The energy accumulated in the vapor is released through condensation to warm a secondary coil containing the water that is circulated through the valence convectors. The process can be reversed in summer to cool the building using the same system and dumping the heat, as Von Arx did, into the groundwater. A special drain system was installed in the building to

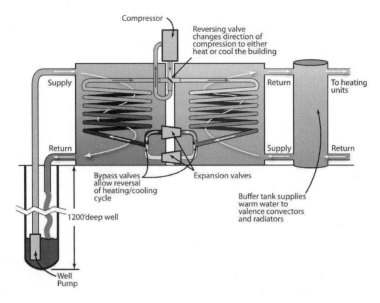

Figure 4.2   The ground-source heat pump. The pump in the well, below the surface of the standing water column, circulates water continuously through the coils of the compressor. The temperature of the water coming from the bottom of the well is about fifty-four degrees Fahrenheit. It is cooled by the compressor to forty-eight to fifty degrees and returned to the top of the well. The heat from the well water is absorbed by the expansion of the refrigerant in the coils on the left from liquid to vapor. The refrigerant enters the coils as a liquid under pressure and is sprayed into a low-pressure zone where it flashes to vapor and absorbs the heat of vaporization from the water. The vapor is then compressed and thereby warmed, and the warm vapor is pumped to the coils on the right, where it is cooled and the vapor condenses again to a liquid. The water surrounding the coils is warmed and circulated to the valence convectors and to other heaters throughout the building. (Courtesy Michael Ernst, WHRC)

collect condensation from the valance convectors when used for cooling in summer.

The system works. The small differences, a few degrees Fahrenheit in water temperature, proved to be enough to heat and cool the building under the most extreme circumstances. The key, however, lies in the remarkably well insulated and tight shell of the building. The energy involved and the cost of operation are surprisingly low, as we shall see below.

ENERGY FLOW IN A BUILDING THAT BURNS NOTHING

Although it proved too early in the solar energy revolution to go off the grid, we planned to generate as much energy as possible on-site without burning anything. The possibility of using hydrogen was dropped as impractical for the building at the time, but it remains a major consideration today as the necessity for reaching beyond fossil fuels moves into the acute phase in this latter half of the first decade of the new millennium. A massive national program for developing solar electric hydrogen with new techniques for storage is one of the most promising routes open to a sustainable supply of versatile energy.

We anticipated that our photovoltaic installation, built as planned, would supply more than forty percent of the annual total institutional energy needs. The cost for the panel system was expected to be $8.57 per watt, installed.

A careful analysis of the relative merits of setting the panels at various angles led to setting them at the pitch of the roof of the new wing, which faces about ten degrees west of due south. The roof has a pitch of eight degrees. The low angle favored the long clear days of summer with the noon sun high and the demand for electrical power likely to be high as well. This arrangement was convenient, allowed best use of space, and would produce an anticipated annual yield of energy that was less than six percent below the maximum possible with the panels set up at thirty-five degrees, an angle often used at this latitude. At such a high angle, however, self-shading in a rooftop installation would reduce substantially the overall efficiency of the limited space. The installation, although extensive, was inconspicuous and did not change the appearance of the building from any perspective except from the air (figure 4.3).

Our installation was designed to feed power into the grid through our own meter. When feeding energy to the grid, the meter runs in reverse, so we are in effect selling power to the power company at our retail rate. No matter the simplicity of the concept or the appropriateness of the arrangements, such matters are never simple and are rarely unequivocally

Figure 4.3 A group of architects took an interest in the building and one of them used a kite-borne camera to take this photograph showing the arrays of photoelectric panels, one on the roof of the porch of the original building and the other on the roof of the new wing. Three hot water panels are visible on the roof of the main building. (Photo courtesy of Charles C. Benton, U. California, Berkeley)

resolved. Our connections to the grid involve a substantial green box in the parking lot that must contain, among other things, a large transformer. It also contains the meter. Long after our installation had been completed and was presumably operating according to the principles all had agreed to, I observed three technicians from the power company hard at work on the green box. I inquired as to their purpose not long after they had started in the morning. The answer had to do with how the metering worked, an interest that I shared. I returned by chance late in the day and, passing them as they closed up the box, indulged again my curiosity as to just how it all worked and whether it was working properly. Their answer reflected, apparently, and for me, alarmingly, a day's frustration in dealing with three meters whose function they could not fathom. I was, of course, no help and my questions did nothing to salve their frustration. For my part, confidence in corporate competence and objectivity in measurements took another blow. Soon after, with Pete Lowell, our local electrical engineer and brilliant analyst—a fountain of insights into virtually all aspects of electricity, hydraulics, mechanics, and philosophy—looking on, we did establish definitively that the meter ran backward through most of the day on sunny days in summer. Our bills appeared to reflect this arrangement whether the technical staff of NSTAR, our local power company, understood why and how, or not. The question remains as to whether NSTAR would pay for energy received from our system beyond the limits of our use. That issue will emerge as critical when the wind turbine, discussed below, enters the system, long delayed, but presumably sometime early in 2009. For the moment, I was much relieved and felt rewarded again for having such competent friends and for insisting on having local technical competence in all matters.

The photovoltaic system was installed in fall 2002. The building was occupied in March 2003, and independent metering commenced in October 2003. The building has proven to be very efficient, both in the conservation of energy and in the production and use of energy.

During the full year from March 2004 to the end of February 2005, the photovoltaic system supplied thirty-two percent of our electrical energy. One could only take pleasure from this experience that confirmed our projections of markedly improved efficiency in use of energy. We used less than one-fourth of the energy as in our previous facilities, where we had done much to reduce energy use, and one-fifth the energy of the national average in other similar office buildings.

Atmospheric burdens of oxides of sulfur and nitrogen, which are common contaminants from power plants, in addition to carbon dioxide, are also reduced by installations such as this one. Reductions were significant, of course, and accrue as a local advantage.

The energy intensity of the Ordway Campus compares quite favorably with two other recently constructed ground source–connected build-

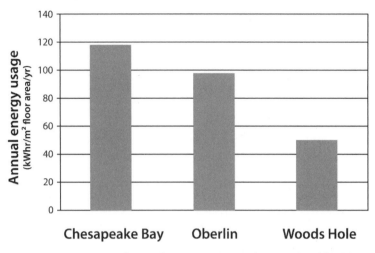

Figure 4.4   A comparison of annual energy usage in the completed building versus other recently constructed buildings that provided background for this project.

ings reported in the Department of Energy High Performance Buildings database—the Chesapeake Bay Foundation headquarters and the Oberlin College environmental studies building (figure 4.4). The energy intensity of the Ordway Campus is forty-three percent of the Chesapeake Bay building and fifty-two percent of the Oberlin facility (not corrected for potential seasonal variation).

The building has a monitoring system for energy consistent with the overall purpose of the institution, research, and education. The data have been available and published continuously online since May 2004.[6] They were used initially, of course, in the commissioning of the building to make various improvements in structure and operation as the building was completed.

A WIND TURBINE

The Ordway Campus's perch on the ridge that forms the backbone of the peninsula gives the campus an apparently favorable site for a wind turbine.

The ridge is approximately eighty feet above sea level, and the turbine, with a tower greater than one hundred feet, would have direct exposure to the southwest winds of the region. Although the site seemed obviously favorable, we thought it wise to establish a tower on the site, close to where we assumed any turbine would be established, and to accumulate data over a year or more on the reliability of the wind.

Later, when we had accumulated data on the wind and had gained sufficient experience with wind turbines to know that we had a reasonable site for a turbine, we turned again to the MRET with a second request, this time to help us to pay for a turbine and a tower 123 feet tall, well above the trees and buildings nearby. At that height we anticipated that a one hundred–kilowatt turbine would produce, with our already installed photovoltaic cells, more electricity than we require at the moment. The excess could be fed into the grid and, during the high-demand weeks of summer, we would be contributing our excess power to our neighbors on Cape Cod. If the rules established by the power companies for buying excess power were not favorable, or if we chose, we might use the excess energy to charge the batteries of a small fleet of electric cars to be used in commuting, thereby displacing another source of heat-trapping gases.

Although there was not much question as to whether a wind turbine would be productive, there was a serious question as to whether a turbine on our site would be an unwelcome intrusion on our neighbors. The questions surrounding need and missions seemed clear enough: a research institution dealing with the Great Issues of Environment in the early years of the third millennium should aspire to competence in supplying its own energy either on the site or by contributing to a communal system remote from the site. The objective was not simply a practical matter of independence—always desirable if possible—but also an example of what can, and quite probably should, be done for all new and reconstructed buildings as a matter of course. But the question of the attitudes of neighbors opened a new set of issues focused largely on sound.

Scientists are respectful of data, but my data and simple assurances that the site was suitable carried no weight at all with my colleagues. We had to have not only the anemometer tower and data on wind but also data on sound. The need for a tower to gather the preliminary data was an invitation for a great deal of further discussion, research, and analysis. How tall? What might be on it? How would it be erected on our site without a giant crane? Would it be safe, once erected? Did we need permission from the Town of Falmouth? Would the neighbors agree that a tower was appropriate?

We did need a permit from the Town of Falmouth for the tower. We notified abutters and held meetings with neighbors. Attitudes varied, of course. Some equated the tower to the turbine and objected to the prospect or the sound of the anemometers as though they were themselves equivalent in potential to the thirty-foot-long blades of the turbine. The permit was issued but not before a special figure was prepared showing the spindle pole of the meteorology tower with its anemometers against the sky, almost indistinguishable behind the maze of telephone poles and wires that dominate the view from the Treetops condominia across the highway from the campus. A tower 105 feet tall to sample the wind was erected using a large crane to set it in among the trees on the approximate site we had in mind for the turbine (figure 4.5).

We operated the meteorology tower for two years. Data were collected at three heights, but, of course, the data from the top were of greatest interest. These data were ultimately pooled as discussed below with data from the National Oceanic and Atmospheric Administration data buoy in Buzzards Bay (BUZM3) to provide a six-year record of the local wind.[7]

The wind turbine experience also included a field trip to Burlington, Vermont, to visit Northern Power, where there is an operating direct-drive machine similar to the one we anticipated purchasing. This machine was installed on a granite outcrop overlooking a giant granite mine, a breathtaking hole, still being worked for granite slabs. As spectacular as this stately wind machine was, turning slowly on that day in a fitfully light wind, the gaping mine next door, with its maze of cables, cable cars, shear cliffs, and monstrous scale, could not help but capture the attention of all and become one of the most memorable experiences of a committee fo-

Figure 4.5   A constructed picture with a view from the road of the wind turbine as proposed and the renovated Hilltop House. The meteorology tower has also been inserted to the right of the turbine.

cused not on granite but on wind. As the weak wind of that moment failed, attention wandered inevitably to the mine. But members of the committee did climb the tower, which had an interior ladder leading to the large nacelle, where there was space enough to view the direct-drive armature which, with no gearing at all, turns almost silently. A wind sensor activates a motor that turns the blade into the wind and keeps it there. When the wind speed increases to a danger point, the sensor applies a brake that stops the blade. The committee was thoroughly impressed with the maturity of the design and the graceful beauty of the machine.

The field trip extended to other wind machines, including a small one constructed on a substantial house lot owned by one of the leading employees of Northern Power. This one was on a simple tower that could be erected with a small winch by one person. At the foot of the tower one could hear sound attributable to the turbine and the vibrations of the tower, but feet away from the tower it was impossible to detect the sound of the installation above the background sounds. A neighbor, however, was objecting vigorously to the wind machine on the basis of "noise" that troubled him. His house was far beyond the circle within which the turbine could be heard in any circumstance, and there was little question but that his objections were other than what he was claiming. No discussion, modification of the wind turbine, or objective data could satisfy such objections.

The extensive wind farm proposed for Nantucket Sound, the Cape Wind Project, started in 2001, has encountered similarly irreconcilable objections, nominally based on environmental effects, but in fact based on personal opposition to the proposition of establishing what are to some aesthetically displeasing wind turbines in that place. Two elaborate environmental impact statements, one of 4,000 pages by the U.S. Army Corps of Engineers and a second 2,000-page report by the Minerals Management Service of the Department of the Interior, have found no noteworthy environmental problem with the 130-turbine proposed installation. But the opposition continues to assert environmental problems as their basis. The reality of implacable hostility does not diminish the need for conscientious pursuit of environmental implications of such installations. We proceeded on that basis through two rounds of environmental reviews of our own proposal for a one hundred–kilowatt turbine.

The site proposed was east of the front corner of the building on, or very close to, the highest point of the Quissett Ridge that is on our land. An engineering consultant specializing in sound prepared systematically measured comparative appraisals of sound around the site. To satisfy ourselves we had to ensure that we had met all requirements of the town and also had the interest and support of the neighbors. Although there are always uncertainties in such undertakings, we found that we had met, or could meet through modest efforts, all requirements for a one hundred–

kilowatt wind turbine with a 123-foot tower on our site.[6] The primary requirement was that if the machine were to fall, it would fall on our land and not on another's.

The MRET made a grant for approximately half the total cost of the Northern Power machine, expected to be about $500,000.

The analyses of energy demands and uses were extensive. The one hundred–kilowatt turbine could be expected to produce sixty percent to more than 140 percent of the total energy use by the building, according to the data available at that time.

We anticipated that the two installations—photovoltaic panels and the turbine—would produce energy throughout the year with the largest amounts during the windy periods of spring and fall.

There were interesting implications of shifting the entire institution from a net consumer of electrical power produced in centralized power plants in the region to a net source of electrical power, however small. This transition is occurring as the region makes the decision on whether to install 130 large wind turbines on Horseshoe Shoal in Nantucket Sound, the now well known and long delayed, Cape Wind Project.[8] This large new source of renewable energy would in fact produce three-quarters of the average current energy requirement of Cape Cod and the islands of Nantucket and Martha's Vineyard. The possibility of shifting Cape Cod from dependence on electrical energy from fossil-fueled plants to major, if not complete, reliance on renewable electrical energy, locally produced, is real. It would take, in addition to the Cape Wind Project, a modest effort on the part of institutions and towns and individuals in conserving energy and in shifting to renewable sources including, as the Center is doing, solar panels and wind, to find the other twenty-five percent of the base load. It is a modest challenge, easily within reach, and it would relieve the region of a major expenditure that is certain to increase as the price of oil and gas and coal rises. The interest is real and contagious. A 1.5-megawatt machine is now being proposed and broadly supported for the technology park in Falmouth, and there is a concerted effort by the Commonwealth of Massachusetts to support the installation of solar panels for power and for domestic hot water.

At this moment, March, 2009, early steps have been taken to start construction of the Center's wind turbine. The tower has been designed and built. When the turbine has been installed, sometime during the next months, the institution will be a net source of electricity for the region, an example of what is possible now and a clear step toward reconstructing a world that is not progressively impoverished by wastes of fossil fuels.

5

MATERIALS, SEWAGE, AND COSTS

Adjusting Our Vision

The public is moving gradually toward recognition that the world is a closed system for most resources, except energy. Suddenly, there is a new set of public responsibilities in protecting the whole, a finite earth, afflicted and collapsing around us with what appear to be infinitely expanding demands on all its resources. Unfortunately, most of the currently vigorous segment of the human population has been taught throughout its formative years that the continued expansion of every aspect of the human undertaking is not only appropriate but essential. And daily news media reinforce that perspective by assuming regular growth in the economy and reporting alarm at any weakness in growth. The corollary of such growth in all facets of human affairs, including especially the human population, is intensified competition for space in the world and resources to live by—greater competition between individuals and greater demand for all resources.

We establish governments to provide broadly acceptable rules (laws) to protect rights of individuals and to protect essential public resources from destructive consumption. As growth proceeds and competition between individuals intensifies, as it inevitably does, the need for rules soars and more and more information is needed for government to do its job in protecting the public welfare. Unfortunately, the assumption persists that the world remains large in proportion to the demands we place on it and can continue to accommodate not only the further expansion of human influences but also the worst we have to offer, including wars. That view persists despite the evidence discussed previously that human-induced disruptions are now measurable from pole to pole and from the depths of the oceans to the top of the atmosphere, and now, beyond that into nearby space.

The fact is that global environmental changes are rendering every organism maladapted to its current environment. The process is leading to universal and progressive failures of the biotic systems that keep the earth working. The increments are at first seen as an inconvenience: a few species are affected, diseased trees are lost, forest fires increase, fish stocks drop. Continued, the impoverishment becomes an economic problem that emerges as a local, but ultimately, global financial catastrophe. Governments, still captured by the infinite growth myth, discover that flexibility in response has been lost as the environment crumbles beyond repair. The Haitian abyss yawns.

Correcting the trend is no simple matter. It requires not only understanding the local issues but also wide acceptance of a new view of the world. The new view starts with recognition that *the biophysical world is small and fragile and operates under rules that govern life itself, rules that do not recognize compromises of air and water and land called forth in the short term to ease strains on government, industry, and commerce. The biophysical rules are as immutable as gravity itself.* They are also not new.[1] They are as old as the biblical Golden Rule.

The climatic disruption is a product of this expansionist dream. There have been and continue to be massive failures of governmental responsibilities. A two-degree Celsius increase in the average temperature of the earth is now advanced as inevitable. "Adapting" to it is essential, the wise folk say. The World Bank has recently published a sixty-five–page report on how to adapt to a warmer earth, as though the warming were going to be finite and comfortable.[2] But two degrees as an average for the world as a whole means four to six or more degrees in the high latitudes of the northern forests and the tundra, both of which hold large stores of carbon ready to be mobilized by decay as temperatures rise. Limiting the temperature excursion to a stable two degrees is not possible, and "adapting" to an open-ended climatic disruption is fanciful in the extreme.[3] Restabilizing the global climatic regime at the twentieth century mean is the only reasonable solution if we are interested in retaining a habitable earth. We have a global emergency, and the world desperately needs new models to compete with the dreams of infinite growth.

In the case of energy the answers as we built this campus seemed reasonably clear and we could do pretty well in tapping renewable sources for our daily use. We could not, however, take into account the energy embedded in the materials used in our equipment and buildings. To the extent that we became a net source of pollution-free energy for the total human enterprise, we were making a contribution toward restabilizing the whole. But we could not eliminate the "waste" problem. Nor could we resolve the growth problem, but we could lay out a pattern for the next century's innovations moving toward stabilizing the global climate and essential qualities of global biophysics.

Waste also had several dimensions as we advanced in thinking about a new campus in this new world. Bill McDonough offered an interesting challenge in announcing that we would build with "silica and cellulose," and in the end, two hundred years down the road, leave no residues that could be identified as exotic to the site. It was a fine objective, but it remains at best an attractive thought, quite beyond practicality in the present world.

We considered seriously an intensified reliance on local materials, especially lumber. That, too, was a forlorn wish, impractical for the size and shape of the new wing designed to fit the site. We were not rebuilding the hilltop, filling the kettle hole, or building a shelf on that steep slope that dropped seventy feet immediately beside the building. The wing of the early design, rectilinear as it appeared, complemented the Victorian house and provided the space we required, but it ignored the contours of the ridge. The redesign offered four floors that followed the contours of the site. That design, the product of contemporary expectations and thinking, once settled in all minds, demanded steel. Pine timbers, large and flexible, were not an option.

As we moved on with construction, a chain of similar decisions had to be made. Studs were metal because modern construction techniques and builders virtually require them. There is no preparation at the time of installation, no measurement, no cutting. A building that relied on local sources of lumber would be a quite different structure, if less expensive in materials, quite likely more expensive in time and labor, and close to the ground. We could, however, continuously emphasize local materials and Forest Stewardship Council (FSC)–certified lumber. This emphasis brought insights and experience in almost every aspect of the construction, as we shall see.

FINISH WOOD AND LUMBER

The frugality and conservatism commonly ascribed to New England but in fact common in rural settings around the world marked virtually all our negotiations and plans. We actively solicited gifts and contributions of various types, and the stories behind them became a part of the project.

My own lifelong interests in Maine through youth and family, residence in York and Orono, a university town where another George M. Woodwell, eighty years previously, had been the Congregational minister, through countless stories told to me as a child by a brilliantly scholarly father, who recalled in sparkling detail the rich experiences of his youth as a minister's son in various towns in Maine in the early 1900s, kept me close to the state and its land and forests. So when it came time to find wood to finish our building, it was natural for me to seek the interests of Pingree Timberlands, the largest private forest land owner and manager in Maine. Tim Ingraham, an active member of the now numerous owners of Pingree and a good friend, responded most generously and donated beautifully colorful maple (*Acer rubrum*) flooring from their lands and mill for the entire building. The Pingree interests had previously completed arrangements to produce their timber under the certification rules of the FSC and were, even as we talked with Tim Ingraham, selling development rights to more than three-quarters of a million acres in Maine to the New England Forestry Foundation, a land trust, thereby committing their land to long-term use as forests for forest products.

The finish wood throughout the building was by choice American ash (*Fraxinus americana*), resawn from large timbers salvaged from a building in Baltimore and obtained by our builder. Shingles and outside finish were western red cedar (*Thuja plicata*) produced under FSC certification.

For the large porches we desired a strong durable wood that would not require intensive maintenance. A tropical wood, ipe (*Tabebuia* spp.), has been widely used, and a shipment was already available in the United States. It was, we were told, from an FSC-certified forest in Brazil. Highly skeptical because we have worked intensively in the Amazon basin for many years, I demanded proof. There was in fact, accompanying this shipment, a documented chain of custody. The shipment was from the Rio Capim in the Brazilian state of Para, where we had done much work with local farmers and were well known. The certification was correct, confirmed, and we purchased and installed the flooring, which was applied with 17,000 stainless steel screws in drilled holes. The certification was, interestingly enough, supervised by a forester, Johan Zweede, whom I had met previously in Santarem, in the central Brazilian Amazon Basin, and talked with at length and enjoyed. He had appreciated my skepticism and my letter, which he had recognized and answered through channels. It is another small world, that world of research and forests and timber and certification and construction. But there is also purpose in demanding proof and insisting on a system that establishes rules that work. We all felt rewarded when we saw the FSC system in operation from land and forest in Brazil to flooring in a research institution half a world away.

Our addiction to wood and local sources led us to explore possibilities for using local sources of lumber for the large tables any such institution requires as an essential tool of its business. In particular we required a large boardroom table for the common space on the main floor and a much smaller table for the library. We had an attractive dream for the boardroom table that involved the use of local lumber of historical interest. The story starts in Woods Hole in the latter part of the nineteenth century when the peninsula was virtually devoid of trees after nearly 300 years of European settlement and 250 years of intensive agriculture heavily focused on cattle, sheep, goats, and horses. One wealthy resident, Joseph Story Fay, thought the peninsula should be reforested and undertook the challenge by importing tree seeds from Europe. Why he picked European trees I do not know. He must have thought them superior to our native chestnut, oaks, pines, and our grand beech. In any case he is said to have scattered his European seeds on Nobska Point, near where he lived, and where my family now lives. The trees on Nobska now include an exotic white oak (*Quercus robur*), the English oak, apparently one of the species imported by Fay. Unfortunately, some of these towering oaks are succumbing to what appears to be a fungus that affects the cambium and is in a short time lethal. I had cut one of these giants on our land and had myself sawn planks from the large butt log that I envisioned as stock for a magnificent oaken table for the Center. The planks, planed in a local lumber yard, had a rough grain and enough imperfections, including signs of their fatal affliction, to discourage their use, despite our interest. In the end the table was built by a local artisan of black cherry (*Prunus serotina*), probably from Pennsylvania, although I was also able to offer black cherry from local sources. Furniture makers prefer their own sources of stock to avoid having to accommodate the types of imperfections we discovered in the local oak. Again, we compromised a preference for local materials to practicality.

An attractive wooden table was also sought to complement the rich wood finishes of the Robinson Library. Although we sought the interest of local craftsmen, we made no connection. At that time modern loggers were salvaging from the depths of Lake Superior logs lost a century ago when the forests of northern Wisconsin and Minnesota were cut and floated in large rafts to mills. Some of the logs sank. The concept of salvaged lumber appealed to us, and we purchased a veneered table made from the salvaged timber for the library. The lumber had come from a birch log, probably yellow birch (*Betula alleghaniensis*).

SEWAGE

Sewage is a global issue, but it all starts at home. The staff of the Center have produced scores of research papers on water and nutrients in nature, and have been primary contributors to the literature on sewage as well as to the problem. The staff are proud of their command of sewage and not at all inclined to yield easily to higher authority on any aspect of the issue.

During my last years at Brookhaven National Laboratory, I had established a major research program designed to determine how best to transform domestic sewage rapidly through natural processes into a safe and wholesome resource.[4] Nitrogen is the big problem: how is the nitrogen in sewage to be removed before it fouls the groundwater, water supplies, and local streams and ponds? The topic is far more complicated than one might wish, and the focus of continued research and discussion in the larger scientific world. It is also a major issue on Cape Cod and in almost every other coastal area around the world.

Nitrogen is, strangely enough, the major element in fertilizer, essential in the successful cultivation of virtually all agricultural crops, and simultaneously one of the most pernicious pollutants of rivers, streams, lakes, and the coastal oceans around the world. Its success in stimulating and supporting the growth of agricultural crops is mirrored in its success in supporting the growth of pestiferous species such as blue-green and green algae in water bodies around the world. Although a minor stimulation of plant growth might be thought desirable in water bodies, a small increase in plant growth quickly becomes pollution as the new organic matter dies and decays and in decaying uses all the oxygen available.

The giant and growing anaerobic zone in the Gulf of Mexico, where no fish can survive, is the product of the accumulation in the Gulf of nitrogen applied in excess to crops in the Mississippi basin and carried by runoff down the river to the Gulf. There it supports the growth of large quantities of rapidly growing plants, largely algae that are not a part of any food web and ultimately die. The metabolism of decay requires oxygen, of course, just as a fire requires oxygen. The meager supplies in the water column are quickly depleted and a dead zone develops quickly where there is so little oxygen that no fish or other animals can survive. The syndrome is increasingly common in scores of sites around the world as nitrogen in sewage joins agricultural runoff and contaminates coastal waters with an overgrowth of such noxious plants. The effect is a major increment in the biotic impoverishment of coastal waters, including the destruction of local fisheries. The cure, where a cure is sought, is the treatment of sewage to remove the nitrogen as well as other nutrients. The treatment is expensive but necessary if the water bodies are not to be systematically and progressively degraded. Cities such as Boston have gone to extremes to build sewage treatment plants adequate to protect their harbors. The contradiction here is obvious: if the treatment of the sewage is good enough to protect the coastal waters, the freshwater released is of high enough quality to be returned to the land to restore the groundwater and other freshwater bodies, potentially to be used again, rather than dumped at sea, thereby depleting the terrestrial resource (see below).

Cape Cod, of course, is not immune to this array of problems. Its source of water is groundwater, which flows from the elevations in the center of the peninsula toward the coast. There is surface drainage as well with drainage basins and short streams, also vulnerable to contamination. Although there are municipal sewage treatment systems, the common domestic system is either ancient cesspools or newer septic tanks, both of which restore filtered water to the groundwater system. Nitrogen in soluble form, largely as nitrate, becomes a contaminant of the groundwater, surface runoff, and, in densely settled places, all coastal marine systems. Innovations in sewage treatment are needed to remove nitrogen in this form. There are two ways. Nitrogen can be captured on the surface in plants, or it can be removed microbiologically by transforming the nitrate-nitrogen to ammonia or nitrogen gas and releasing it to the atmosphere. The full transformation to nitrogen gas, which is not reactive and makes up about eighty percent of the atmosphere, is, of course, preferable, although more demanding.

The staff was intrigued by the success of John Todd, our neighbor, in developing sewage treatment systems in plastic tanks using aquatic plants, fish, and a once-through flow. He calls the system a Living Machine, and it has been adopted for use in various places around the world, including the new environmental studies building at Oberlin College in Ohio, mentioned earlier. Surely, our small flow of sewage could be captured experimentally and treated on-site using a variety of interesting and promising techniques that could be demonstrated locally and potentially used by others. But sewage, of all topics, must be treated according to code, and the code is strict. The best we could do in escaping the narrow restrictions of a conventional septic system and drainage field was a denitrifying system called the Ruck system, that had been approved by the town and was designed to last indefinitely. It was expensive, but our engineer, experienced in working with the Town of Falmouth, could shepherd our proposal through the town successfully and was eager to proceed. The cost of our system would be about $30,000, much higher than I had anticipated, but a sure way of controlling the nitrogen and versatile enough to allow some experimentation. We proceeded with the change.

Months passed as the construction moved on. Then one day a large bulldozer appeared on the front lawn and began the excavation for the Ruck system. The excavation expanded, and questions were asked. The code was invoked; the hole had to be deep enough to drain sewers on the ground floor, already below the surface in the front of the building. The auditorium was the problem. It could hold up to one hundred people, and the code called for a much larger system to serve that many people. More than that, we had determined that the system should be a gravity system. The whole installation had to be below the building. So the bulldozer plowed on, scraping earth up from a giant hole covering an acre or more for the half acre of gently sloping bottom devoted to the Ruck system. The scrapings were piled beside the road. The pile became mountainous and the hole cavernous. The Ruck system had expanded under the code to a large installation, perhaps the very largest anywhere. The hole and the pile brought comments about how the center of gravity of the whole earth had shifted and its rotation had actually slowed due the lower angular momentum of earth from the depth of our hole piled so high along the road. And the cost had soared as well. No one dared speculate officially, but a factor of ten seemed modest. No one had raised this issue to offer a chance to review the needs and to connect the real need for sewage treatment with the size of the hole. Intensive as it was, the director's scrutiny did not extend to a regular review of the sewage system and another battle with code.

Months later, after the building had been occupied and operated for some months, the Ruck system was not working properly and the experts were puzzled. The details, never hidden, only overlooked, came forth. The design and construction, following the leadership of engineers, not biologists, demanded a daily flow of 1,575 gallons based on an assumption of seventy-five gallons per day per thousand square feet of floor space plus three gallons per day per capita in the auditorium, designed initially for one hundred occupants. When the auditorium was compressed to save money, the sewer system was not reduced correspondingly. The actual daily flow from the building was 150 gallons or less, a tenth or less of the assumed potential. Fortunately, we could bypass part of the system and restore the function in a fractional segment of our grand code-designed sewage plant. Although we were not put to the test, we had confidence that, left to our own designs, we would have accommodated all our sewage on the surface with a much simpler and far less expensive combination of systems. But the code, in protecting the public, could not and did not allow experimentation or innovation with sewage treatment, even within our own land.

The code went on to plague us further, and the experience stands as a warning to all who venture down this difficult road. Our wet chemical laboratory migrated in the design to the top floor of the new wing as the modest auditorium, reception area, and kitchen area settled at the ground level. The design of the laboratory received careful scrutiny from all, including of course the scientific staff and the code officers of the town. The questions had been many, and they had been answered to the satisfaction of all. How would the wastes be controlled to avoid contamination of the Ruck system and the groundwater? What would be disposed of in the sinks? How would acids and other noxious chemicals be handled? We explored the concept of a closed-system, waste-free chemical laboratory in the context of the Center's research. It met mixed reviews from the staff, some of whom were intrigued and some of whom found it awkward to the point of outrageous. Would we be able to avoid careless disposal in the sinks well beyond our plans for complete containment of wastes? Could we ensure safety by strict rules? Or should we have hold-up tanks for each drain backed up by a central tank in the basement to ensure that all wastes could be contained and treated properly before any disposal? What material should be used in the drains? All these questions were answered in the planning phase and reviewed by the town's code officers. But they arose again late in the construction phase.

An eye-wash station with a floor drain was essential, a discovery made well after the floor and the plumbing had been "finished." The drainage system had to be built to accommodate chemical spills and uses not previously envisioned by the officers interpreting the code. The iron drains, previously approved and installed according to the plans, would have to be replaced with chemically inert plastic all the way to the ground floor, where a limestone-filled tank would neutralize acids. Again, there was no discussion or amelioration short of rebuilding the drainage from sinks to the tank in the basement, despite having to open the walls and floors again and refinish all. It was the code, and the delay and expense were all a part of construction. Such costs were covered by our contingency fund, so wisely established and managed by Robert Barry, our chief financial officer. Innovations in construction were not possible, whatever the plans or wishes of the owners.

WATER, TOILETS, AND YANKEE INDEPENDENCE

Early in our considerations the question arose as to whether to use composting toilets. The decision had some profound implications. Using them
would greatly simplify the sewage treatment problem and be consistent
with our minimalist objectives, both in the treatment of sewage and in the
use of water. After all, using potable water to flush away sewage is an ex-
travagance in any context. But there were some problems. The composting
toilets require one or several tanks in the lower floor fed by large diameter
(ten inches or more) pipes that descend directly, without any deflection
from the vertical, from the toilets above. The tanks and pipes take up valuable interior space and require periodic maintenance. Also, the pipes from
upper floors command space directly below on lower floors. The pipes in-
troduce yet another complexity in design and in construction. Their existence limits flexibility from floor to floor and takes up interior space. The
system requires a continuously running fan that maintains a negative air
pressure to avoid odors in the building. If electrical power fails, there
can quickly be a serious problem. The continuous removal of air from the
building puts another burden on the heating system not easily accommodated through our enthalpy wheels. Finally, I found myself contem-
plating what I might do when, just prior to the board dinner on a Sunday
evening, a distinguished guest and generous donor quietly but urgently inquired about retrieving her watch dropped in a careless moment from the
third floor toilet into the maw of the composting tank in the basement. I
decided to have low-volume flush toilets. It was a big decision.

Flushing toilets with water generates a substantial flow of sewage, and
building codes take over in defense of the public interest. The fundamental
issues are not new, but remain troublesome. In the sparsely occupied agrarian landscape of the nineteenth century, sewage could often be handled
simply with relative safety and the water restored to the groundwater system locally without expensive treatment systems and without conspicuously contaminating water supplies. With intensified use of the landscape,
especially in towns, centralized collection became necessary, first by dump-

ing the untreated sewage, usually into nearby water courses or into the coastal ocean. The "treatment" in that instance was dilution followed by natural processes that filtered the water and either consumed the organic matter through decay, or deposited it as sediment. The process required space, land, and water, but each of these was available and the treatment was inexpensive and effective, at least within limits deemed acceptable at the time. As human settlements spread and densification proceeded, demands for "treatment" intensified. But in the end, even "treated" sewage was finally released to nature for the final purification before the water was again available for human use. The local experience was in this context and instructive.

The village of Woods Hole as late as the mid-1970s had a sewage collection system that had served large segments of the village for many years. The pipe dumped the untreated sewage directly into the harbor, where strong tidal currents quickly diluted and dispersed it. As the village grew, the collection system expanded and the wisdom of dumping ever more sewage into local waters used for fishing and clamming and recreation drew significant attention. The scientific community included at that time four independent laboratories and a wide diversity of technical competence in dealing with water and human interests. The competence included oceanographers specifically involved in research on nutrient elements, especially nitrogen; fisheries scientists; ecologists engaged in studies of toxic substances; and broadly talented staff of the U.S. Geological Survey.

The discussion was intense with the specialists in nutrient control of algal growth asserting that the sewage, rich in nitrogen, was enriching the coastal waters and good for the fish and fisheries. Others pointed to experience with toxins showing that even very small quantities of fat-soluble substances such as DDT, that are not very soluble at all in water, are accumulated in any fat-body on the basis of solubility alone. Food webs, moreover, as we learned above, concentrate such substances further, and concentration factors may run to hundreds of thousands–fold above environmental levels.[5] Low concentrations of such toxins exist in most sewage in this industrial world. The ecologists argued that it was bad policy to set up circumstances in which toxins of any sort, including toxic concentrations of nutrient elements, or even very small quantities of metals such as mercury or cadmium, were released into coastal waters. The arguments grew shrill, even bitter on occasion, with one side asserting that there was benefit in releasing untreated sewage into the waters and the other asserting that it was simply crazy for a scientific community such as Woods Hole to consider for a nanosecond dumping untreated sewage, or for that matter, treated sewage, into the coastal waters anywhere, let alone their own harbor and favorite fishing spot.

My own contributions to this discussion at that moment were quite limited, but experience left no doubt in my mind as to how the issue had to be resolved. The experience with DDT and radionuclides had shown definitively the potential for environmental mechanisms to move substances around in the environment and to concentrate them in surprising places. In retrospect the information about concentrating factors in nature should not have been surprising at all, for there is universal recognition that plants concentrate nutrient elements such as nitrogen and phosphorus from low concentrations in water and soils and pass those elements and many others on to animal populations, including the various organisms of the human food web. It should not have come as any surprise that fat-soluble poisons such as DDT and other chlorinated hydrocarbons with various biotic potentials would be concentrated as well from very low concentrations, even below easily detectable levels, to toxic levels in places far removed and with effects never originally imagined.[6] Sewage is never pure. It inevitably accumulates toxins of various types—lead from pipes, cadmium in small quantities from various sources, household poisons, medical refuse, and virtually every noxious substance that enters the market in any form. And it accumulates surface runoff from roads and buildings and work sites of all sorts as well as whatever is washed from the air in precipitation and then washed from the land. By that time scientists and the public had considerable experience with radioactivity distributed globally and the details of the circulation and hazards of radioactive elements such as cesium and strontium were well known. There could be no question as to the hazards of various toxins in sewage.

Insufferable academic and political discussion among intransigent factions became intolerable, and the directors of the various institutions wisely took matters into their own hands and decided the issue. The Town Fathers, and ultimately, the voters agreed. The expanded collection system in Woods Hole would be redirected out of the coastal water to a sewage treatment system on land. The village was connected to a pipe through a pumping station and the sewage was pumped to a treatment area in North Falmouth. There the ultimate treatment was, at least immediately, the spray irrigation of a forest with sewage that had received "primary" treatment (removal of solids). Research had shown that if the rate of application of sewage to a forest were low enough the forest would retain the nitrogen and organic matter. The rate of application did not have to be very much above the normal precipitation level, however, for the nitrogen to break through and be carried into the groundwater.[7] But the immediate problem was removed from the village.

The new problem was how to get the water safely back into the groundwater system uncontaminated with nitrogen. Not surprisingly, the common solution, as was in use in North Falmouth at the time, was to release the partially treated sewage into nature for the final stage of treatment. Again, the system works as long as the demands are small relative to the area available for restoration of the water. We have with sewage, interestingly enough, acknowledged responsibility for restoring the water quality, but we have regularly dodged the ultimate responsibility by transferring the problem to another place and to nature for the final purification. Although we acknowledge de facto the need to have more space available to support civilization than we normally assign to our settlements, we regularly compromise that space in favor of continued growth of the human undertaking, and in so doing, commit the world to a further increment of chemical disturbance, a chronic disruption that accumulates as progressive impoverishment. The fact is that we take up more space in the world with our biophysical needs than we are willing to acknowledge and continue down the path of compromise and intensified chronic environmental erosion. We are back to the central point of the Center's efforts in establishing its new campus. Eight or nine acres would seem to offer considerable freedom to devise ways of indulging a New Englander's propensity for independence in managing essential resources, especially water. But I was dreaming again. Municipalities see a larger challenge.

As intensification proceeds, the volume of sewage increases and its character changes. Municipal sewage systems receive entirely new classes of wastes from industries that focus their profits and spread their costs into the public realm. Ideally, stewardship of the environment would demand that water used for human purposes be restored in quality and replaced by its users into its normal pattern of flow, thereby maintaining normal flows of both ground- and surface water. If the problem is limited to the ordinary flow of nutrients and organic matter from domestic uses of water, local treatment systems can be used effectively and safely. As the quantity of sewage increases and its quality changes with industrial development, the requirements for treatment expand beyond reason. Practicality, convenience, economic considerations, and political compromise have commonly ruled, leading to highly permissive standards and serious local pollution problems. Industrial wastes can not be accommodated in municipal treatment systems but are a part of the cost of business and must be treated in-house. Even so, treating modern municipal wastewater to make it safe for reuse as a water supply is difficult, expensive, and never foolproof. Treatment is usually partial, even in the most advanced systems, and ultimately results in a release to natural systems that in fact complete the process before the water is again taken for human use. Acknowledging that fact seems essential, and planning it into our system for *a world that works* is essential.

The big decisions in water management are made in a political context, usually with a series of compromises to lubricate the entire process. Codes are used to define local management of sewage. The codes, although they may protect the public interest, at least in part, often also stifle innovation, require large investments, and substantially fix patterns of land and water use forever. Unfortunately, we have allowed this system to go too far without regulation, and we have landscapes locked into a pattern in which untreated, or poorly treated, wastes are made public property and dumped into an environment that can not handle them. And our commitment to eternal growth in all aspects of the human endeavor ensures that the problems will become worse. Local pollution soon becomes global, and the world slides down another notch on the scale of impoverishment.

Real estate interests have often been allowed to determine the density of housing and thereby the intensity and patterns of use of land and water without any consideration of biophysical limits or costs. Municipalities are left to find the cure *ex post facto*, to build sewage collection and treatment facilities and to dispose of the wastes. Municipalities with access to coastal waters find the disposal of wastes there inexpensive and convenient, even if treatment is required. And the construction industry, fed with new business on a continuous basis, is of course pleased.

On Long Island, New York, for example, the municipalities on the south shore established a district sewage agency for Suffolk County, the eastern two-thirds of the island. The Southwest Sewer District was established in the 1970s to build the collection and treatment systems as well as a series of outflow pipes across the beaches to dump the effluent from this densely developed region into coastal waters.[8] The obvious objective, of course, was to protect the groundwater and later, the beaches, from contamination by sewage. The groundwater was the major source of water for most households, which tapped it with shallow wells easily produced by driving a "point," a porous pipe, into the surface water table of the sandy glacial sediments. Sewage was initially disposed of in cesspools, which ultimately, in high density areas, contaminated the groundwater. There are many other sources of contamination of groundwater in densely populated areas, and removing the sewage is no assurance of safety. Worse, speeding a massive transfer of freshwater from groundwater into the sea reduces the source, potentially lowering it beyond the reach of shallow wells. At that point a new central water supply system is needed, tapping either an abundant exotic supply such as that of New York City, which uses a very large drainage basin in the Catskills, or deeper, glacial water, still uncontaminated and abundantly available, at least for the moment. So it was in the Southwest Sewer District. These were, of course, grand engineering projects that required new digging, new pipes, and new deep wells, all at public expense. Corruption seemed pervasive despite the efforts of some excellent political leaders at that time.[9] The failures were at every level, from regional planning that allowed far too intensive use of the land and water resources through the concept of centralized treatment with large treatment plants fed by complex collection systems with pipes laid on every street, to the outfall pipes that deposited the sewage off the beaches of Long Island in the coastal ocean. The system immediately produced a need for a central water supply with a new set of pipes in every street and new sources, a construction firm's Valhalla, and a prodigious new public expense generated originally by irresponsible real estate development and total lack of concern for management of water supply and disposal of sewage. The effect was to improve and stabilize a new, necrotic landscape, another large region that depends on vastly larger regions of land and water to supply essential resources and purify its wastes. The cause was the gross failure of regional planning that initially allowed the sale of small lots and dense development without consideration of future needs for such elementary fundamentals as water supply and sewage management. Purchasers of lots acquired not only a small lot but also, in ignorance, large future mortgages to water and sewage.

So it has been and remains elsewhere. In the much older municipality of Boston during the late 1970s and early 1980s the harbor was obviously burdened with sewage. The water supply problem had been resolved many years earlier through a large drainage basin that feeds the Quabbin Reservoir in western Massachusetts. But the municipal sewage problem had grown with the city and was acute. It was ultimately resolved by constructing a single giant treatment plant in Boston Harbor. The sewage was treated to the point of innocuousness and released into Massachusetts Bay. Ideally, freshwater so treated would be clean enough to be replaced in the supply system on land rather than dumped into the sea, thereby eliminating the possibility of contamination over time of the coastal waters with trace contaminants that escape the treatment system. But the convenience of sea dumping appeals when the costs of returning the water to the land for potential reuse are considered. Again, a large necrotic landscape calls on a much larger area of land and water to restore the resources it has exploited. As such necrotic regions expand, their tentacles touch and tangle, and the world runs down.

So how would we at the Center manage water if we had our way to avoid such municipal crises? Our objective would be minimal intrusion on the normal flows of water in the region. But the building itself is an intrusion, an impermeable surface that deflects the approximately thirty inches of rain that fall regularly in this region each year. And our presence has generated other impermeable surfaces such as a paved driveway and part of our parking lot. But, we thought, we have several acres to work with, ample land to accommodate our needs for a water supply and for restoration without intruding on neighbors or town.

First, we might make use of the water that is already displaced by the building, catching and retaining it as the primary supply. The total area of roof, including porches, is about 8,100 square feet. If the average annual precipitation is 2.5 feet, the total water available from the roof is slightly more than 20,000 cubic feet or about 151,000 gallons annually. That would make available about six hundred gallons per day if use is restricted. The actual water use in the building over four years (table 5.1) is approximately equivalent to the water from the roof.

Second, the deep well designed into the heating system ensured that there would be water from a more or less conventional source to supply all the building's needs, which are in fact quite modest. There appeared to be no reason to have a connection to the municipal water supply, thereby incurring both a significant continuing financial cost and a further dependence on municipal services. We learned, however, that such independence is not appreciated. The Falmouth Fire Department requires that there be pressure at all times in the sprinkler system, not dependent on a local electric pump. They demanded an eight-inch pipe from the town's supply line in the street. Again, there was no discussion possible. We could, if we

TABLE 5.1   Annual use of water over five years. These summaries do not include water collected from the roof and used in irrigation.

Period	Amount (gallons)
2/27/04–2/25/05	93,500
2/25/05–2/24/06	158,600
2/24/06–2/23/07	142,100
2/23/07–2/15/08	104,700
2/15/08–2/20/09	103,372

wished, have water collected from the roof and stored in tanks for whatever use. We could have a deep well with an abundant supply if we chose. But neither innovation would satisfy the fire department, who insisted on a large, direct connection to the town's system and positive pressure continuously in the two sprinkler systems described previously. The well would be for the heating and cooling system, no other purpose. All water withdrawn would be returned and there would be no net withdrawal. Drainage from the roof could be captured and stored if we wished, but our interest in self-sufficiency for water moved none of the regulators. To obtain potable water from the roof would have required filtration to remove any contamination picked up on the roof. But the wash-water and water for flushing toilets would have been used untreated and released from the Ruck sewage treatment system, nitrogen- and organic matter–free, to the groundwater at no cost to the town or the institution beyond maintenance of the system. In the building as constructed the drainage from the roof irrigates lawn and gardens nearby, except for water captured and stored in a 1,200-gallon tank for later use in irrigation if needed. Building codes and the requirements for fire protection ruled out any more venturesome approaches, our most imaginative dreams notwithstanding. Rules and laws and customs and codes become fixed over time and constructive innovations in land and water use become limited. We were challenging a worldview that had impregnable standing in law.

THE COST OF GREEN

In the era of cheap oil, when only a few scientists were much concerned about the disruption of climate globally and before there was more than talk about the distant point of peak oil production, there was little basis for arguing that saving oil by building solar sources of energy was economical or even wise. A colleague at the University of Minnesota managed to worm from me an appraisal of the cost of a large array of solar panels I had designed and built in the 1980s with my son to heat our leaky old summer house in Woods Hole. My Minnesota friend followed conventional wisdom, applied discount rates, considered alternatives, the current and future prices of oil, and the discounted value of PhDs and students working as carpenters and plumbers, even on an educational venture, and announced to the world with great humor and all the pleasure that such analyses bring to colleagues and students alike that I was regularly spending $3.60 to save a gallon of oil, then selling for fifty to sixty cents. He was correct, I suppose, but the heating system still works and has worked for the last twenty-five years, heating our house for eight to ten months annually and providing all the domestic hot water for much of the year. And our reduced dependence on the oil company provided personal satisfaction rivaling that of my colleague William Von Arx, who smiled for years at the frustration of his gas company when his use of gas dropped.

Now I am asked just how much the special considerations of energy and beauty and comfort added to the cost of the new quarters for science on the Ordway Campus. The response is awkward. What is the standard? The immediate issue is usually the short-term cost, the cost of the building at the time of construction. Our objective, however, was to look to the future and to build for it. The conservation of energy was a large issue and led to a long-term perspective. Twenty years seemed reasonable and an increase in the price of oil seemed inevitable in that period. But beauty and comfort are real enough and affect potential in attracting and holding a distinguished and proud and effective staff. History and experience, however, were not much help. Scientists, environmental scientists in particular, have been pleased to occupy just about any quarters at all even in major scientific enterprises such as the national laboratories, where modern environmental research enjoyed an enormous boost in the post World War II years. There is hardly any low limit on the costs of housing based on that experience.

I remember well, for instance, the quarters provided for what was then probably the largest, and certainly one of the most vigorous and best financed institutes for environmental research in the 1950s and 1960s. It was at Oak Ridge National Laboratory on the facility's extensive site in the Tennessee hills. The Environmental Studies program had been established in the mid-1950s and represented a bold new departure for the Atomic Energy Commission, which had not had a great deal of experience with, or interest in, the subtleties of environmental science up to that time. Such innovations are always delayed long beyond the need and established under emergency circumstances. This new venture was no exception. It was a sudden reaction to the global environmental embarrassments surrounding the U.S. tests of nuclear weapons in Nevada and in the Pacific, and money flowed freely. There was no time to plan new quarters for this substantial new scientific program. It had to fit onto a laboratory site hastily built during the war and already full.

The immediate solution was pragmatic and practical, a solution from the war less than ten years back: a large, galvanized iron culvert called a Quonset hut, named for a military establishment in Quonset Point, Rhode Island. The military establishment had designed highly efficient and inexpensive housing by burrowing into culverts. The culverts did not necessarily have to be buried; they could be built above ground. The Oak Ridge culvert was mostly above ground and had been improved by adding a door at one end and windows, fitted awkwardly into the curved, corrugated, galvanized iron sides. Abundant, inexpensive energy from oil and coal heated it in winter and cooled it in summer. Efficiency was not a consideration. Shelter was.

Ten years later this troglodytic burrow was still the den of ecologists working on the compelling issues surrounding the many aspects of the development of nuclear energy in war and peace. The research was pioneering a new realm, exciting, vital to human welfare (at least we thought so), and being carried out by scientists accustomed to field conditions. A well appointed culvert was a big advance beyond a tent: a luxury, inelegant, but in the climate of the Tennessee hills, comfortable enough, serviceable, and inexpensive. Should that be the standard for comparison?

We, working in Woods Hole in a new institution forty years later, were in a new time and a new world. The environmental researchers at Oak Ridge soon moved into more conventional quarters appropriately designed to support their work. But the memories of the many early years of make-do quarters and equipment survive and stand in sharp contrast to the needs of this moment in the new millennium as we look toward the end of the age of fossil fuels and toward a new world of enduring sources of energy and innovations in architecture and construction only dreamed of earlier. We were dealing with this new world and on quite different terms from the postwar era of the 1950s and '60s.

All buildings are compromises among personal and institutional interests, beauty, comfort, utility, practicality, competing dreams, and costs in time and money. They are also expressions of the personalities engaged at that moment and prevailing tastes and perspectives in architecture. All decisions are set within a budget more or less arbitrarily determined by trustees and interested donors and friends. In the most rational of contemporary nongovernmental worlds an early step in the planning for a large capital expenditure is a careful feasibility study carried out by an outside agency that charges a high price for exploring the interest and potential of friends and donors for generating the money. The feasibility study has the putative advantage of generating interest and momentum among potential donors as well as offering an estimate of what might be possible. Negative feasibility studies are nonexistent. If there is any real question as to the result, there is no point in the study. Our superficial analysis of the scale and wealth of our clientele was that the prospective supporters that a professional team would turn up were far too modest in number and capacity to justify the expense of asking. It would be much better to get busy and build the building and find the funds as we proceeded. Blindly confident and with a most supportive and confident board of trustees, we marched on to music written by our own staff and played from our own trumpets. We were very much strengthened in this decision by a promise of a million dollars from trustee Gilman Ordway at about this time and various other gifts from trustees.

The objectives were compelling and became more so as we proceeded with designing a building we thought ought to cost about three million dollars. Internal committees worked, trustees discussed, architects visited, and we traveled individually to see the buildings of Oberlin, Gap headquarters in San Bruno, California, and a John Abrams building on Martha's Vineyard. We examined the building we had purchased and judged it worth working with as we used it for meetings and savored the freedom owning it gave us. Finally, at an unforgettable meeting of our board of trustees in the commons of Gilman Ordway's Fish Creek Ranch in Wilson, Wyoming, we came to the unanimous agreement that we would proceed with William McDonough at a cost estimate that was pulled from the air, the wildest of guesses based on what we thought we might find in financial support, and what we thought we might need to meet our expectations. The next step was into a far higher realm of reality as architects went to work.

Committees convened and reviewed as architects worked. New architects came into the firm and joined this project, each introducing innovations that had to be reviewed, modified, and adopted. Finally, we reached the limit when offices were "regularized" late in the planning by a new architectural face in an effort to equilibrate space in an irregular building among the staff who were no less irregular in needs and expectations. It was time to get a formal price on our dreams. Professional estimators familiar with contemporary pricing do such things. We were too high, much too

Figure 5.1 All appreciate the spacious and comfortable common space at the juncture of the new and old. (By permission, Judith Watts, Bronxville, NY)

high, and some economies were appropriate. We shrank the wing, reduced the size of the auditorium, and squeezed the offices. And we went to the trustees for license to do what was needed as opposed to what we had originally planned. It was granted with the same enthusiasm the trustees and staff had generated in dreaming that far. The product appealed to all and justified the enthusiasm (figure 5.1).

We were in fact engaged in an experiment, a test of what can be done now in improving the quality and efficiency of construction with materials easily available at prices most can afford. If the initial price were to drift too high, it would not be an appropriate example, at least as some saw the issue. On the other hand, a reduction in the cost of operation over years may justify a substantial investment in improved construction. Potential increases in the cost of energy for heating and cooling are difficult to appraise, but those costs are in any case large at current prices and, over a twenty-year period, justify a substantial investment in economy. A building that is carefully constructed to be tight and well insulated is essential, and the marginal cost of such care in construction is the difference between competence and sleaze. It was not an issue as far as we were concerned. Although we were as frugal as they come, we were not building a Quonset hut under emergency conditions. Nor were we letting the lowest bid define the issue. And we were in a position to define and demand competence in all realms.

Our objective from the beginning was operation without on-site combustion of anything, at least directly in heating or cooling. Cost was an issue, but continuing on a one-way, one-time trip for civilization through an obviously limited resource whose use was poisoning the earth and disrupting climates globally to the point of driving civilization off the earth was not something a rational world might want to plan—or having advanced on such a course, celebrate and continue. We saw a duty to provide an example in a new direction *now*. And we thought we saw a way and hoped it would prove contagious.

A ground-source heat pump would require electricity, but no on-site use of fossil fuel. Electricity could be produced directly on the site from solar panels and from wind. Both are expensive but both operate indefinitely, once installed, at low maintenance cost and without cost for the basic resource. Both are also a part of our experiment, both are open currently to subsidies in Massachusetts, and both are being developed rapidly now. Our course was clear and, although the cost of installing solar panels and a wind turbine would push our costs above the range we had set for ourselves initially, those accounts could, and would, be handled as the experiment they are. The final costs will appear after twenty years when we

TABLE 5.2 The cost of the project before occupancy in March 2003, excluding wind turbine. Interest charges for loans before and during construction were added to capital costs.

Description	Land	Building	Capitalized interest	Total
Purchase price	$254,000	$506,000		
Construction		7,381,000	270,000	
Total	254,000	7,887,000	270,000	
Total project				8,411,000

have the data on the actual cost of fossil fuels over that time and the cost of commercial electricity in the same period.

The final cost of construction, including the purchase price of the land and Hilltop House, was about $8.4 million (table 5.2) without the wind turbine but including the solar panels and the hot water system.

The completed cost, excluding the cost of the land and the original building and furniture, was $340–350 per square foot for a very comfortable and attractive building whose operating costs for energy, including heating and cooling, are less than ten percent of the costs of other buildings of similar size and purpose. The cost of oil, ever fluctuating and certain to be taxed in various ways, will always exceed the cost of sun and wind and will make the effort in shifting the heating burden to enduring sources of energy an obvious financial, as well as environmental, success.

6

THE PRODUCT

A Campus that Works . . .
and a World that Might

The spores of that puffball of dreams we met at the door of Hilltop House in 1998 are already spreading locally and beyond, feeding discussion of the emergence of a new world. It is not quite the world built on "silica and cellulose" in the dream of Bill McDonough, but the movement is palpable and exciting. Energy is the core, but we reach with the new building and its campus much beyond the mechanics of energy to infect the staff and associates with pride, confidence, and contagious vigor.

Locally, we are pleased as an institution to be released from a complete dependence on fossil fuels. We have a campus that burns nothing, produces thirty percent of its total electrical demand, and will, with a wind turbine, soon to be installed, produce excess power that will contribute to the Cape's electrical grid and might be harnessed to power small electric cars used in commuting to work. Beyond our immediate interests, we can see how all of Cape Cod could within a few years become substantially independent of fossil fuels for its electrical power and for much of its transportation. To be sure, such independence would require the wind farm proposed for Horseshoe Shoal in Nantucket Sound as well as many highly efficient buildings supported by solar panels and wind turbines. But the success of the Ordway Campus shows that these thoughts are not dreams. They are a map into a new world that is on its way. And we like the looks of it.

Globally, there is far to go and much to do. Architecture and construction are simple matters. Shifting national energy supplies to wind and other renewables is a big political, cultural, and economic as well as physical challenge. It entails building a new worldview, a new perception of public purpose. Suddenly, biophysical facts of a finite earth emerge as a transcendent public interest rivaling, even controlling, economic and political interests. Accommodating those newly defined limits will require more latitude for experimentation and innovation than we found open to us.

That is the core message of the Woods Hole Research Center as it pursues its research on how the biophysical world works. Designing and building its new campus was part of our business, our own contribution and as much of a research project as anything the institution has undertaken. And it was rewarding beyond our dreams. The rewards flowed to the staff and trustees and the architects and builders, all of whom joined in the experiment and took delight in the process of reviewing, testing, and learning. It was a full-time exercise in government, diplomacy, politics, economics, and, once construction began, the mechanics of energy—its conservation, storage, production, and use.

So what is it that we want of this new world?

The Ordway Campus is an attempt to reach for the antithesis of the conventional world view, a perspective that has been framed over the last century and a half by abundant and inexpensive fossil fuels, especially oil. Prior to the fossil fuel age, the primary dependence for energy to support civilization was direct or indirect access to the sun, land area, and agriculture, including forests, supplemented by wind and water power. Now as we approach and pass the peak of abundance of fossil fuels and realize that their use is, in any case, poisoning this civilization and must end, we discover again the ancient ways of capturing the flows of solar energy and improving on them with new technology. We realize the persistent elemental truth that land (and water) area offers access to solar energy and durable, simple, inexpensive ways of capturing and using that energy. And the patterns of land use that might seem reasonable for a fossil-fueled economy, now seen as urban and suburban sprawl, are not necessarily appropriate for the new world of renewable energy systems. Looking both ahead and back we discover that the medieval patterns of land use, preserved in European landscapes, with villages surrounded by agricultural land and forests, have much to recommend them, at least from the standpoint of preserving essential qualities of landscapes and the potential for exploiting renewable energy. We are, however, constrained by the context of the current time as we push hard toward a new context that must quickly evolve. Worldviews are challenged.

A recently published book by J. G. Speth and P. M. Haas, entitled *Global Environmental Governance,* starts with a "thought experiment" involving the imaginative assumption that the reader is the first person arriving on the earth, the first to encounter the full abundance of life that the earth held prior to the explosive human incursion of recent time.[1]

Speth and Haas capture in that one suggestion the ecologist's model of the world, built and maintained over all of time by life itself. The economic-political models are all shunted aside and the world is seen for what it is—a biophysical system whose parts are living systems, the product of evolution—each one, each individual, each population, each species, each landscape, and Earth itself, all obviously successful in the propagation of life. If we were to set out once again from that first moment of arrival, knowing what we know now, how would we proceed?

We might reflect on possibilities and decide that what works, and has worked for eons, might be worthy of recognition and preservation. The thought, of course, is not new. It has roots in written history that dates to ancient Greece and before. In our own time ecologists like to observe with Aldo Leopold and others that the first principle of intelligent tinkering is to save all the parts. The concept is the core of contemporary ecology, the very heart of the study of the human habitat. As we contemplate our campus as a step toward rebuilding *a world that works* we might examine that world through the mental experiment of Speth and Haas. That world at the beginning of the explosive human invasion of Holocene time, perhaps the past 10,000 years, was exclusively composed of individual and collective successes, survivors of the endless game of evolutionary roulette that has made the atmosphere what it is, the land, the oceans, the forests, all the plants and all the animals, including those who became modern humans. Scientists dissect that four- or five-billion year process of biotic evolution and identify critical points that produced the present physical and chemical environment, an atmosphere of mixed gases including about twenty percent oxygen, eighty percent nitrogen, and trace quantities of heat-trapping gases that substantially fix the temperature of the whole earth and define the qualities of life that can survive.

The central point here is that keeping the world working is, on the one hand, a simple matter of restoring a system that builds and runs itself. On the other hand, the objective becomes saving the whole, not just the shards left after greed has fractured the whole. Societies organized around self-aggrandizement and greed require elaborate bodies of rules to preserve the common interest in a viable whole. The whole is atmosphere, land, water, climate, plants, animals, and environmental chemistry everywhere. The whole is now not only an economic and political system, but also a stable and nurturing global environment. What is demanded is not merely a series of technological inventions, but, even more importantly, a new way of thinking about the world and managing human affairs to preserve the whole—a new philosophy. The new way of thinking, however aggressive, does require new tools, new technologies, that preserve and do not destroy the world. The challenge is large, for unfortunately this civilization has expanded to affect the whole and the expansion continues, so far, by design. Corrections now require a reconfiguration of the current concept and structure of civilization starting at its philosophical roots and extending into every corner of a now corporately dominated world committed to continued growth.

We found an architect who has taken a tree as his model and tried to redesign the built world to transform wastes into feedstocks and eliminate toxins by building with "silica and cellulose." The task is futile in the pragmatic eyes of most, but the effort in thinking through the cycles of nature and how we have entered them, fractured them, and spoiled our own lives gives us a basis for resolving what will work in fact, and what will not, in the new world that is here now, and the newer world that is coming. Architect McDonough forced scientists to rethink objectives and to realize the limitations of even the most aggressive of their own efforts at reaching for a better way. "Less bad" is still bad, as McDonough and Braungart point out.[2] A change in the entire framework of civilization is called for.

Our world was once, just a few hundred years or so back, forested over forty-four percent of its land surface and it is now forested over only twenty-eight percent of its surface, give or take a bit. Much of that forest is now sparse and presents a vastly different target for the continuous flood of radiant energy from the sun. Its color is different and its reflectivity is different and its water budget is different and its climates are different. Amplifying those differences undermines all that has come before and built the habitat for all life. Preserving that life as the machinery that keeps the habitat working is the new objective. Restoration and preservation are the touchstones of success. Further disruption accentuates the impoverishment, a suicidal course.

It is a monstrous challenge, this biophysical dilemma. Suddenly the world questions tried-and-true methods of accumulating profits and wealth in a primarily capitalistic world. Garrett Hardin brilliantly articulated the issues in various publications over more than three decades,[3] and various scholars have more recently expanded on them.[4] Profits accrue most abundantly, of course, when the costs can be pushed out from the industry into the environment and made public property, shared by all, while the profits are retained by a few. The economic pressures are great and require, in fact demand, governmental regulation to protect the public's interest in a habitable environment. In a world that is closing in on us, that governmental function moves to the center and becomes the core of governmental purpose. Our mission is serious business. And time is short.

Along the way we have stumbled through various compromises, among them the concept of "sustainable development."[5] That phrase was invented to placate the expansionist aspirations of economists and politicians and corporate executives who learned their trades when the world was in fact large and appeared to be large enough to accommodate virtually any insult. Further development in the same pattern that has already pushed the world into a cascade toward impoverishment is hardly a step toward sustainability. Many, perhaps most, of the world continues to have great difficulty in accepting the sudden transition to a "full world,"[6] or even the sense of the phrase.

The "suddenness" is characteristic of the expansion of the human enterprise at this phase in its growth. It is in large part due to the expansion of the human population, an exponential growth that is nothing short of explosive. The population globally is now about 6.8 billion people, almost twice the number on earth just forty years ago and more than three times the number at the end of World War II in 1945. But the expansion is not mere numbers, although the numbers are serious enough.

Technology has also expanded and spread globally. As a result each individual now has the potential to command for personal purposes far more of the earth's resources than any person of any earlier time. The technology makes each individual larger, and those in the technologically advanced nations such as the United States and the nations of western Europe take up more space and resources than those in less developed nations. The growth that we see is not the mere doubling of the human population, it is that doubling amplified in its effects by the invention, expansion, and spread of technological development that gives each individual, each corporate interest, greater capacity to use the surface of the earth to institutional or personal advantage. The automobile is a good example, with its engine of tens to hundreds of horsepower, its ton and a half of steel, its speed, the roads it commands, and the air and water and space it commands, not to speak of the fossil fuel mined and refined and delivered around the world for one individual. The combination of expanding numbers and greatly expanded capacity to capture space and resources produces a doubling time of environmental effects measured, not in decades, but in years. Along with this growth has come an illusion of wealth and soaring aspirations among these swarming new inhabitants of the planet. I say "illusion" because the costs of this expansion of human activities are pushed into the common environmental pool and not tallied. It is the classical case defined so brilliantly by Garrett Hardin of exploiting the commons at public expense while pocketing the personal or institutional advantages. The costs, however, do not disappear. They accumulate as local, regional, and ultimately global necrosis and impoverishment.

Presumably, in the circumstance postulated by Speth and Haas in their book, the scientific community, entering this new self-sufficient world with the insights we now have, would have proscribed in the beginning the systematic poisoning of the world, changing the composition of the atmosphere, or the energy flows, or the circulation of water, or air, or nitrogen, or calcium, or the color, and therefore the reflectivity, of water or land. We would, presumably, on the basis of first principles, have avoided setting up industries that based their existence on consolidating resources for narrow purposes, focusing profits, while spreading expenses and wastes broadly across the public spectrum. A petrochemical industry based on mining carbon-based fuels for energy and releasing the waste products, toxic particles and gases, into the atmosphere to circulate widely would be unthinkable. So would spreading persistent, broadly toxic poisons to control specific organisms that are judged to compete with human interests. Our challenge in developing a new campus would have been much different, simpler and less difficult by far.

We are not of course starting from the beginning, as Speth and Haas proposed, but the model we aspire to is the same. Our challenge now is to rebuild the human enterprise *ex post facto* to fit an earth that has become obviously degraded and is quickly sliding into further impoverishment illustrated abundantly around the world by such surging environmental, political, and economic catastrophes as Haiti, Central Africa, drought-stricken Australia, our own Southwest, northern Mexico, and now New Orleans, the Gulf Coast, the Central Valley of California, and the bark-borer–devastated forests of southeastern Alaska, the Rocky Mountain states, and Canada.

The most threatening political innovation now in response to the climatic disruption is the rapid shift to a drumbeat of support for "adaptation" to the "inevitable" changes in climate already entrained, as though those changes were minor inflections of climate to a new steady state, irreversible and easily accommodated. They are neither minor nor likely to be stabilized in any time of interest to those now living unless we take explicit action to control the composition of the atmosphere immediately.

The correction required is drastic, the immediate removal from current emissions of at least five billion tons of carbon annually for the globe as a whole. Five billion tons is approximately the annual net accumulation of carbon as carbon dioxide in the atmosphere in these early years of the new millennium. It is about fifty percent of the total emissions produced by human activities, including deforestation and the burning of coal, oil, and gas. The balance beyond the five billion tons of carbon is absorbed into the oceans and plants on land.

Such a transition is possible. The objective of atmospheric stabilization has already been defined in the Framework Convention on Climate Change, signed in Rio de Janeiro in 1992 and subsequently ratified by more than 180 nations, including the United States. It is only the first step, designed to stabilize the composition of the atmosphere, not the global climate. The treaty, now national and international law, requires implementation and must ultimately be followed by an actual reduction in the atmospheric burden to restabilize climates globally.

Our objective in building a campus that burns nothing is a serious matter, an example to be followed widely and applied incrementally to whole regions such as Cape Cod and the world. But we have to do more. We have two tools: management of forests and restrictions in use of fossil fuels. Both are necessary. Globally we need to preserve all remaining primary forests, a step that will remove about 1.6 billion tons of carbon annually from current emissions. We can, and must, reestablish forests on existing, once forested land, now impoverished. If we can establish these new forests on 360,000–720,000 square miles, we will store annually about one billion tons of carbon, a major further contribution toward stabilizing the atmospheric burden and ultimately returning to climatic stability. An approximate one-third reduction in global use of fossil fuels as those changes in forests are implemented will remove the five billion tons of carbon from current annual emissions needed to stabilize the current atmosphere. Further action in the same realms will be needed to reduce the heat-trapping gas content of the atmosphere to lower levels and restore long-term stability to climates.

With the forest issue in mind we have dedicated a fraction of our property in Woods Hole to restoration of forests under the watchful eye of a local conservation agency. About two-thirds of our total of about nine acres is in forest, with more than 2.4 acres permanently committed to conservation and under the management of a local land trust.

The building and land use that have evolved under these various constraints of energy, purpose, place, and funds have come as close to a pinnacle of perfection as is possible in the current context. Functionally it is what we sought, a building that is efficient in use of energy as planned, comfortable in all seasons, draft-free, well lighted with natural light in day and efficiently lighted at night. It is handsome, even attractive, from every angle outside and offers a limitless array of attractive views internally. It is a showpiece with tours arranged regularly for visitors led by staff who are proud to display their knowledge and experience with a technically complex building. As such it is a teaching tool, and the staff, pleased with their association, are all teachers; several, in fact, are independent experts in solar energy systems and contemporary innovations in construction.

Although these innovations by the Center are attractive and essential, they are incomplete in that we have not freed ourselves from a dependence on fossil fuels except for those normally consumed in daily work life. The fossil fuels used in the construction of the equipment we use daily, the energy embedded in that equipment through manufacturing, is large and real. And the energy we use in our scholarly business of traveling for research and teaching is no less real. Air travel is a major consumer of oil, and the emissions associated with long trips by air overtake the small savings made in more efficient lighting and heating. A world of very low emissions of heat-trapping gases will be a world in which air travel is expensive and very much limited. But it will also be a world in which buildings and entire campuses are self-sufficient for energy on a day-by-day and year-by-year basis and in which it is common for net production of energy locally to exceed immediate needs and for the excess to be stored or shared with others.

How might we have improved our performance within the rules we had to work under? There were, of course, some possibilities that seem now obvious. There may have been a far more satisfactory and far less expensive resolution to the sewage issue if we had addressed it more comprehensively and aggressively, starting much earlier, although the details of what could have been invented and accepted by the town are not clear.

We now have more than five years' experience with the building, enough to test our initial optimism and to detect flaws and trends. There were some flaws, some unexpected leaks where wind-driven water found its way around door and window casings, but the incidents were few.

A loss of power in a winter storm confirmed the institutional dependence on power from the local electrical grid and raised the question of a local auxiliary power source to accommodate such emergencies. The topic has been discussed and explored extensively around the concept of cogeneration, using a small diesel generator whose normally wasted heat would be captured to heat the building. However, the emergency was contained without difficulty even in midwinter. The building is tight, well insulated, and held its heat. It was in fact heated for several days once, when the groundwater heating system failed, with the electric heaters that had been installed in the hot-water tank to back up the solar hot-water panels. Although the need can be acute when power is lost, the number of occasions is very low indeed and it has not seemed necessary to install a large emergency generator.

In one realm we made a significant miscalculation. The expansion of demand for computer equipment has exploded beyond anything we had dreamed of or could have known. The explosion is in part technological in that the potential for equipment has expanded and we have been greedy participants in the expansion. It is also in part due to our own aspirations in science. We have drawn in scholars who are heavy users of large-capacity computers that have heavy demands for energy and release much heat. The facilities in the basement room devoted to computer servers have expanded far beyond any concept we had entertained at the time the plans were drawn. The result is an unexpected need to dispose of the excess heat generated in those small quarters. There are two solutions. First, in cool weather of fall, winter, and spring the excess heat can be used directly in the heating system either through a heat pump or directly as hot water. When that is impractical or impossible, as in summer, the server-room can be air conditioned using the well water as the heat sink. That use of the well warms it with heat recaptured in winter, just as William Von Arx captured summer heat stored in the gravel beneath his house. Far more promising from an energy standpoint, however, is the replacement of older servers with newer equipment that uses much less energy, a transition that is underway.

We remain creatures of the technological world, increasingly dependent on the flow of technological innovations into science. At the same time, the innovations are liberating and enabling. We have the capacity now to capture solar energy in new ways locally and to use it without corrupting the world or even our neighbors' immediate interests. And our neighbors have the same capacity. The trends can feed on themselves, enabling even further consolidation of influences and further independence.

In a wisely run world, massive governmental and industrial efforts would have been underway for three decades to conserve energy in buildings and travel and to develop new local sources of renewable energy and methods for storing it. The new Obama administration of 2009 seems poised now to lead in encouraging these steps, so long delayed. There is also gradually developing an interest in industrial and manufacturing methods that are far more energy-efficient and make use of local sources of renewable energy. At the same time there will be in this new world parallel efforts to close up industrial and domestic systems to protect the integrity of global chemistry and avoid progressive toxification from careless chronic or sporadic releases. That program might take the Ordway Campus as a model and develop a massive effort to deflect the currently disastrous course of climatic disruption through solar-based hydrogen production and use. It will not be the same world run by a new fuel. It will be a new world, with new perspectives designed to raise human aspirations far above a course clearly bound for misery with teeming billions at or below subsistence levels on an eroding planet to life in a green global garden with a potentially infinitely renewable future.

That is the only way the new world can be made to work, as a global park designed to preserve all the species for all of time.

There are ancillary benefits to building as we have done at the Ordway Campus, not the least of which is simple pride among a talented staff who are pleased to work in an attractive building that stands as a model of institutional purpose. And they take delight in spinning out the stories attached to virtually every element of the building and its furnishings. Inquire about the floors and hear of the Maine Woods and our various longtime connections there that are expanding their influences to preserve forests in parks and to ensure the preservation of as much as a million acres of managed forest as well. Ask about the carpets that protect the floors in critical places from time to time and learn about The Shaw Company, where they have pioneered nontoxic dyes and methods of recycling used carpet materials into replacement carpet, a model industry for the new world. Bill McDonough memorialized this style of recycling in the title of his book, *Cradle to Cradle,* and arranged for the carpets to celebrate the building and become a part of the building and its story, which moves quickly into visions of the new world.

So where are we going from here?

Yes, the Haitian Abyss yawns.

But it need not be the new world.

The elements of a new departure are falling into place. The Ordway Campus of the Woods Hole Research Center is one glimpse into the plan. There are many others, including the brief view set out by Speth and Haas as their "thought experiment"—the ecologist's model. Whatever the source, the requirements for the survival of civilization are clear: the physical, chemical, and biotic structure and their functional integrity as part of the biosphere are essential requirements. The new world is a park, and the new rules defend its biophysical integrity. It is a human world of closed systems: "wastes" are resources or they are not produced. The overriding political objective and the purpose of government is recognition, definition, and protection of the human habitat, that thin skin of the earth that supports life.

Cassandra sits in high places today, and there are many ways to speed the slide into the Abyss. But there is one clear way to build *a world that works*—one piece at a time.

NOTES

PREFACE

1. Hawken, P. *Blessed Unrest: How the Largest Movement in the World Came into Being and Why No One Saw It Coming* (New York: Viking, 2007).

CHAPTER 1

1. Economists such as Herman E. Daly, who have pointed to the contradiction intrinsic in the concept of infinite growth into a finite world (Daly, H. E. *Steady State Economics* Washington, D.C.: Island Press, 1991), find little support among either other economists or politicians, most of whom continue to feed the engines of growth as the primary basis of human welfare. Daly quotes Alexandr Solzhenitsyn as advocating "a zero growth economy . . . Economic growth is not only unnecessary but ruinous" (1974). J. G. Speth, in his new book *The Bridge at the Edge of the World* (New Haven: Yale University Press, 2008), devotes a section to the necessity for looking toward a stable society, relieved of "growth" in the contemporary context, and calls attention to earlier classics by John Stewart Mill and others, who also have pointed to the absurdity, nay, the impossibility of, infinite growth into a finite world. The growth envisioned in these treatises refers to the open-ended expansion of demand on physical and biotic resources, which are in fact finite. See also Holdren, J. P., G. C. Daily, and P. R. Erhlich, "The Meaning of Sustainability: Biogeophysical Aspects," In M. Munasinghe and W. Shearer, eds., Defining and Measuring Sustainability: The Biogeophysical Foundations (Washington, D.C.: World Bank, 1995).

2. McHarg, I. *Design with Nature* (New York: John Wiley and Sons, 1969).

3. Biotic impoverishment involves the progressive erosion of the capacity of land and water to support human needs. The processes are widespread globally. They have been defined for natural communities in Woodwell, G. M., ed., *The Earth in Transition: Patterns and Processes of Biotic Impoverishment* (Cambridge, UK: Cambridge University Press, 1990).

4. P. R. Ehrlich has recently exposed once again the fallacies of rampant expansion of the human population into a finite realm: "Demography and Policy: A View from Outside the Discipline," *Population and Development Review* 34 (1) (March 2008): 103–113.

5. See Woodwell, pp 3–11 and Woodwell et al. pp 393–411 in G. M. Woodwell and F. T. Mackenzie, eds. *Biotic Feedbacks in the Global Climatic System.* Oxford University Press, New York, 1995.

6. Intergovernmental Panel on Climate Change (IPCC), Climate Change 2007: Synthesis Report Intergovernmental Panel on Climate Change. Fourth Assessment. (Cambridge, UK: Cambridge University Press, 2007).

7. The earlier reports have led to a widespread assumption that the world will be well served and safe if we can hold the buildup of heat-trapping gases in the atmosphere to the equivalent of 450 parts per million (ppm) of carbon dioxide in air and the average warming of the earth to two degrees C. Although the actual carbon dioxide content of air in 2007 was about 382 ppm by volume, we had already passed the 450 ppm equivalent in heat-trapping gases. And the upward drift of temperature already entrained by the present atmospheric burden will almost certainly carry the temperature rise to two degrees or more. A two-degree rise in the average temperature of the earth is a devastating six or more degrees in the higher latitudes and ensures paralytic droughts in normally moist sections of the continental tropics. Worse, the rise in temperature triggers feedback systems that result in still higher levels of carbon dioxide and methane in the atmosphere from the destruction of forests, the accelerated decay of organic matter in soils, and the reduction in the capacity of the surface water of the oceans to hold carbon dioxide as a gas, among other factors. Holding the rise to two degrees is probably not possible in this circumstance.

8. R. A. Houghton, pp. 28–34 in Woodwell, G. M., *Forests in a Full World* (New Haven: Yale University Press, 2001).

CHAPTER 2

1. Woodwell, G. M., and E.V. Pecan, "Carbon and the Biosphere: Proceedings of the 24th Brookhaven Symposium in Biology, Upton, NY," 1972. (U.S. Atomic Energy Commission, 1973).

2. Woodwell, G. M., and F. T. Martin. "Persistence of DDT in Heavily Sprayed Forest Stands," Science 145 (1964): 481–483; Woodwell, G. M. "Toxic Substances and Ecological Cycles, Scientific American 216(3) (1967): 24–31.

3. Dr. Ramakrishna joined our staff almost by accident. He had been at both Harvard University and the Woods Hole Oceanographic Institution as a Fulbright postdoctoral scholar, and I managed to draw him onto our staff for a year while his wife completed a graduate degree. We had no money at that moment, but he accepted the challenge of research on a new international convention on climate change. Money did come, and his activities ultimately led, under U.N. auspices, to the Framework Convention on Climate Change. His key role in that highly successful treaty continued through the entire process of negotiation, the signing at the Rio Earth Summit meetings of 1992, and the development and support of the Kyoto Protocol in 1997. Dr. Ramakrishna later (2006–2009), on leave from the Center, served as policy advisor to the executive director of the U.N. Environment Programme in Nairobi, Kenya.

4. Richard H. Backus has shown that the early English settlers from the southeast coast of England brought with them the common use of the term "hole" for coastal bays or passages on their native coast. He speculates that "Wood" came from the name of a settler in Sandwich, Massachusetts, who was venturesome and may have assigned the name himself in writings of that first century of settlement. Backus, R.H., *How Did Woods Hole Get Its Name?,"* Falmouth Enterprise (Oct. 16, 2007), 4.

5. Mann, C. C., *1491: New Revelations of the Americas Before Columbus* (Viking, 2006). Williams, H. V., "The Epidemic of the Indians of New England 1616–1620 with Remarks on Native American Infections," Johns Hopkins Hospital Bulletin 20 (1909): 340–349.

6. Conklin, E. G., in Lillie, F. R., *The Woods Hole Marine Biological Laboratory* (Chicago: University of Chicago Press, 1944), p. 24.

7. Ibid.

8. Lillie, *The Woods Hole Marine Biological Laboratory,* 15–23.

9. Lillie, *The Woods Hole Marine Biological Laboratory,* 31.

10. Marsh, G. P., *Man and Nature* (New York: Charles Scribner, 1864); revised and published as *The Earth as Modified by Human Action* (New York: Charles Scribner's Sons, 1885), a better known and more widely circulated version of this distinguished scholar's major work.

11. Woodwell, G. M., R. Revelle, G. J. Macdonald, and C. D. Keeling, "The Carbon Dioxide Problem: Implications for Policy in the Management of Energy and Other Resources. A Report to the Council on Environmental Quality," *Congressional Record* July 26, 1979, 125 (104): 1–6. Also published in *The Bulletin of the Atomic Scientist* 35(8): 56–57.

12. Woodwell, G. M., *Forests in a Full World* (New Haven: Yale University Press, 2001).

13. That experiment defined the pattern of disruption of an oak-pine forest caused by a gradient of chronic exposure to gamma radiation (similar to X-rays, but higher energy). Although chronic, high-intensity gamma radiation is unusual and probably not a normal factor in the evolutionary history of the biosphere, the pattern of response was systematic and familiar. It followed the patterns defined elsewhere by other chronic disturbances, including especially the gradient of exposure to climatic extremes at higher elevations in mountains, the transitions to tundra in high latitudes, and the gradients of disruption of forests caused by oxides of sulfur and other pollutants from smelters in Canada and Russia. The most resistant life forms in all cases were low-growing, small-bodied, rapidly reproducing forms such crustose lichens and mosses. Polyploidy (extra sets of chromosomes) conferred resistance to chronic disturbances of many types, including ionizing radiation. Trees were vulnerable in all instances, some, of course, more than others. Some trees, including those species such as pines that have a small number of large chromosomes, were especially vulnerable, about as vulnerable to acute exposures as humans. But the important point was that the pattern of change in the structure of nature was universal, similar around the world. And we later realized that it applied as well in aquatic systems. The term "biotic impoverishment" was formulated and the gradients of impoverishment, once described, could be seen and the stages defined virtually everywhere on land and in water bodies around the world. Impoverishment had already advanced far globally and become the rule. Examples of intact communities were becoming rare. Woodwell, G. M., ed., *The Earth in Transition: Patterns and Processes of Biotic Impoverishment* (Cambridge, UK: Cambridge University Press, 1990).

14. Todd, N. J. A Safe and Sustainable World: The Promise of Ecological Design Chapters 10–12. (New York: Island Press, 2006).

CHAPTER 3

1. Davis House, owned by the Center; Laurence House (adjacent and leased for our use); Fisher House and the Exchange Building, both on Church Street and leased from the Church of the Messiah; and the Senft Laboratory on Nobska Point.
2. Woodwell, G. M., "On Toxins and Toxic Effects: Guarding Life in a Small World," in W. Draggan, S. Cohrssen, and R. Morrison, *Preserving Ecological Systems: The Agenda for Long-term Research and Development* (New York: Praeger, 1987).
3. Woodwell, G. M., "On Causes of Biotic Impoverishment," Ecology 70(1) (1989): 14–15.
4. Woodwell, G. M., "Toxic Substances and Ecological Cycles," *Scientific American* 216 (3) (1967): 24–31.

CHAPTER 4

1. Extensive hearings were held in Congress in the late 1970s and through the 1980s in which the climatic disruption was defined and predicted with substantial accuracy, although the information available was much more tentative than now. See for instance, "Effects of Carbon Dioxide Buildup in the Atmosphere; Hearing before the Committee on Energy and Natural Resources, United States Senate, April 3, 1980" to which I provided extensive testimony entitled "The CO_2 Problem, 1980." The alarms sounded in those years triggered a response from the fossil fuel industry designed to undermine in the public's eye the scientific data and conclusions that led to predictions of global climatic disruption as a result of continued additions of heat-trapping gases to the atmosphere. The effort involved tens of millions of dollars from Exxon-Mobil and others applied to public expressions of uncertainty and doubt as to the accuracy of the science. The efforts also exaggerated the costs of correcting the trends. The efforts found sympathy in the Reagan and in the two Bush administrations as well as in Congress, where all steps toward reducing reliance on fossil fuels were blocked

for two decades. Gelbspan, R., *The Heat Is On* (Cambridge, MA: Perseus Books, 1997); Mooney, C., *The Republican War on Science* (Cambridge, MA: Perseus Books, 2005).

2. ASHRAE/IES Standard 90.1 – 1989.

3. Energy Information Administration, "Commercial Building Energy Consumption and Expenditures, 1999," August 2002, Table C8.

4. LEED refers to "Leadership in Energy and Environmental Design," a system for measuring the quality of construction with special reference to the conservation of energy. The system was under development by Robert Watson of the Natural Resources Defense Council as we moved into the planning and construction of the Ordway Campus, and it was not clearly applicable to our challenge in salvaging an existing building. We were persuaded that our own analyses of appropriate designs were at that time well ahead of the LEED considerations. As LEED matured, a retroactive attempt to conform in detail proved inappropriate.

5. For technical details of such systems, see Kavanaugh, S. P., and K. Rafferty, *Ground Source Heat Pumps. Design of Geothermal Systems for Commercial and Institutional Buildings* American Society of Heating, Refrigerating, and Air-Conditioning Engineers, Inc. (Atlanta, 1997).

6. See Woods Hole Research Center, "Real-Time Building Energy Flow," http://whrc.org/building/education/EngFlw2.asp.

7   The height of the tower was a compromise. Our appraisals suggested a wind speed of 12.0 mph at nacelle height of 130 feet. The increase in output of the 100 kW turbine would be from an estimated 120,000 kWh/yr at 98 feet height to 160,000 kWh/yr at 131 feet, a thirty percent increase in yield.

8. Williams, W., and R. Whitcomb, *Cape Wind* (Philadelphia: Perseus Book Group, 2007).

CHAPTER 5

1. George Perkins Marsh published his "last revision" of *Man and Nature*, an 1864 book, in 1885 under the title *The Earth as Modified by Human Action*. In that edition he provided comprehensive notes summarizing earlier observations of destructive human intrusions into, and callous destruction of, the natural order of the earth, confirming that his own observations

were far from unique or unusual, merely a continuation of notes of scores of predecessors on the erosion of the human circumstance. All felt clearly threatened in their own times. We are, a century and a half later, far more seriously afflicted and far more shrill. See, for instance, Speth, J. G., *The Bridge at the Edge of the World* (New Haven: Yale University Press, 2008).

2. Cantrell, J., ed., "Environment Matters at the World Bank: Climate Change and Adaptation," (World Bank: Washington, D.C., March, 2008).
3. Repetto, R. *The Climate Crisis and the Adaptation Myth* (New Haven, CT: Yale School of Forestry and Environmental Studies, 2008).
4. Woodwell, G. M., "Recycling Sewage through Plant Communities," American Scientist 65(5) (1977): 556–562.
5. Steingraber, S., *Living Downstream* (Cambridge, MA: Perseus Books, 1998).
6. Woodwell, G. M., "Toxic Substances and Ecological Cycles," Scientific American 216(3) (1967): 24–31.
7. Woodwell, G. M., "Recycling Sewage through Plant Communities," Orbit (1997).
8. Suffolk County-Southwest Sewer District: State University of New York, Stony Brook. Special Collections and Archives. Floyd S. Linton Collection.
9. Harrell, J. "Down the Drain," Long Island Business News July 21, 2006.

CHAPTER 6

1. Speth, J.G., and P. M. Haas, *Global Environmental Governance* (New Haven: Yale University Press, 2006).
2. McDonough, W., and M. Braungart, *Cradle to Cradle* (New York: North Point Press, 2002).
3. Hardin, G., "The Tragedy of the Commons," Science162 (1968): 1243; Hardin, G., *Living Within Limits: Ecology, Economics and Population Taboos* (New York: Oxford University Press, 1993). Hardin, especially his "Tragedy of the Commons," remains a very powerful influence in analyses of resources and government. See, for instance, Ostrom, E., et al. "Revisiting the Commons: Local Lessons, Global Challenges," Science 284 (1999): 278.
4. Speth, J. G., and P. M. Haas, *Global Environmental Governance* (Washington, D.C.: Island Press, 2006).
5. Bruntland, G. H., *Our Common Future* Report of the United Nations World Commission on Environment and Development. (United Nations World

Commission on Environment and Development: Oxford University Press, 1987).

6. Daly, H. "From Empty-World Economics to Full-World Economics: A Historical Turning Point in Economic Development," In K. Ramakrishna and G. M. Woodwell, eds., *World Forests for the Future* (New Haven: Yale University Press, 1993).

Index

Page numbers with *f* refer to photos and illustrations, those with *t* refer to tables.